Fragments of Victory

'Activists in movements and the left often feel despair because they have never experienced successful mass struggles – unlike the Republic of Ireland. In 2014–16 working-class communities stopped the introduction of water charges through widespread direct action, while 2018 saw mass participation win abortion rights in the teeth of church power. Written by activists, this book tells these and other key stories of Irish movements and left groups as a key resource for struggles elsewhere.'

—Laurence Cox, author of *We Make Our Own History: Marxism and Social Movements in the Twilight of Neoliberalism*

'A partisan work in the best sense of the term. The authors' sympathies only sharpen their critical analysis of the left's victories and defeats. There is much to learn here for those who seek to understand and change the world.'

—Paul Murphy TD, People Before Profit

'This book captures the sheer energy and diversity of the Irish left at grassroot level and in key campaigns around housing, abortion rights, and public services, bringing clarity to a movement that is rarely given space to explain itself in the mainstream media.'

—Conor McCabe, researcher and editor of *The Lost and Early Writings of James Connolly 1889–1898*

Fragments of Victory

The Contemporary Irish Left

Edited by
Oisín Gilmore and David Landy

First published 2025 by Pluto Press
New Wing, Somerset House, Strand, London WC2R 1LA
and Pluto Press, Inc.
1930 Village Center Circle, 3-834, Las Vegas, NV 89134

www.plutobooks.com

British Library Cataloguing in Publication Data
A catalogue record for this book is available from the British Library

ISBN   978 0 7453 4875 9   Paperback
ISBN   978 0 7453 4878 0   PDF
ISBN   978 0 7453 4877 3   EPUB

This book is printed on paper suitable for recycling and made from fully
managed and sustained forest sources. Logging, pulping and manufacturing
processes are expected to conform to the environmental standards of the
country of origin.

Typeset by Stanford DTP Services, Northampton, England

Simultaneously printed in the United Kingdom and United States of America

In memory of
Alan Mac Simóin
(1957–2018)

Contents

Acknowledgements

We started this book as a series of discussion meetings in 2019 to analyse the Irish left after the 2008 financial crisis and we continued post-pandemic with a reading group on international responses. We would like to thank everyone who presented at and who attended these discussions for shaping our ideas on the subject.

We would also like to thank those who organised and took part in the movements that are discussed in this book. Without them not only would there be no reason for this book but Ireland would be a worse place to live.

We would also like to thank David Shulman and all at Pluto Press who have helped bring this book to fruition.

Finally, we would like to thank those who contributed to and supported this project. In particular we would like to thank Clíodhna Bhreatnach, Kevin Squires, Aileen O'Carroll and Roxanne Hugenberger.

Timeline

2008	**25 September**	Ireland declares it is in a recession
	29 September	Bank guarantee. State agrees to bail out insolvent banks
	14 October	First austerity budget
	22 October	25,000 students and pensioners protest the budget
2009	**30 January–22 March**	Waterford Crystal occupation by workers made redundant
	21 February	100,000 attend ICTU demonstration
	26 February	Civil service strike against pension levy
	25 March	ICTU call off general strike planned for 30 March in order to enter talks with government
	7 April	Emergency budget – NAMA announced
	5 June	Local elections – Fine Gael and Labour do well at expense of Fianna Fáil. Sinn Féin stagnate, radical left gains several seats
	4 August	Gardaí arrest workers occupying Thomas Cook offices in Dublin
	24 November	250,000 take part in one day public sector strike
	21 December	NAMA established
2010	**2 May**	Greek bailout and riots
	11 May	First of four Right to Work marches organised by Socialist Workers Party (SWP) as unemployment hits 14 per cent
	15 May	Éirígí demonstration at Anglo Irish Bank attacked by Gardaí
	18 May	Anti-capitalist bloc at Right to Work march – develops into 1% Network
	6 June	Croke Park agreement between unions and government

September	Ireland unable to borrow in international markets
3 November	Gardaí attack c. 35,000-strong student protest
27 November	100,000 attend ICTU demonstration
28 November	Troika bailout agreed
29 November	United Left Alliance (ULA) formed as electoral alliance
7 December	Only 1,500 attend Budget Day protest at the Dáil
10 December	Community groups and NGOs organise first Spectacle of Defiance and Hope – c. 600 attend
2011 **25 January–11 February**	Tahrir Square Protests topples Egyptian dictatorship
25 February	General election – Fianna Fáil and Greens decimated. Labour and Fine Gael gain seats and form government. Sinn Féin and radical left gain some seats
15 May	15 M Movement in Spain
17–20 May	Queen Elizabeth II visits Ireland, protests organised by republican groups
27 June	First ULA national conference in Liberty Hall
17 September	Occupy Wall Street starts
8 October	Occupy Dame Street starts in Dublin (until 8 March 2012)
15 October	Occupy Cork and Occupy Galway start
27 October	Michael D. Higgins (Labour Party) elected president. Labour wins by-election in Dublin West
3 December	1,200 at second and last Spectacle of Defiance and Hope
14 December	Dáil votes to introduce Household Charges
15 December	Campaign Against Household and Water Taxes (CAHWT) launched
16 December 2011– 24 May 2012	Vita Cortex occupation in Cork by workers made redundant

2012	21 January	Development Aid NGOs set up 'Anglo – Not Our DEBT' campaign
	28 January	Unlock NAMA conducts one-day occupation of vacant NAMA building in Dublin city centre
	24 March	2,000 attend CAHWT rally at National Stadium in Dublin
	31 March	8,000 at CAHWT march to Fine Gael Ard Fheis (national conference). Figures reveal only half the population have paid Household Charges
	14 April	Gardaí pepper-spray CAHWT demonstrators at Labour National Conference in Galway
	31 May	EU Fiscal Compact Treaty referendum passed 60 per cent to 40 per cent
	12 July	First meeting of Irish Choice Network, that later becomes Abortion Rights Campaign (ARC)
	2 October	Workers and Unemployed Action Group leaves the ULA
	29 September	2,500 at first March for Choice
	28 October	Savita Halappanavar dies after being refused lifesaving abortion. Protests follow throughout Ireland and abroad
	12 November	12,000 at Waterford hospital protest
	24 November	12,000 at CAHWT and Dublin Council of Trade Unions anti-austerity march
	5 December	Local Property Tax introduced to replace Household Charges
2013	19 January	ARC officially formed
	26 January	Socialist Party (SP) leaves the ULA
	9 February	50,000 attend ICTU demonstrations around the country. Rows between CAHWT and stewards in Dublin
	Spring	CAHWT occupations of council chambers and revenue offices
	16 April	Croke Park 2 agreement rejected by trade unions

June	90 per cent Local Property Tax compliance. CAHWT disintegrates
1 July	Unions accept Haddington Road agreement
30 July	Legislation enacted that allows abortion when the pregnant woman's life is at risk
August 2013–June 2015	Squat City established in Grangegorman, Dublin.
7 October	Coalition to Repeal the Eighth Amendment (the constitutional amendment banning abortion) formed
15 December	Ireland exits bailout programme
2014 February	Water meter installation blocked in Togher, Co. Cork – the first action in the Water Tax campaign
23 May	Local elections – Labour and Fine Gael do badly. Sinn Féin and radical left do well. Ruth Coppinger (SP) elected in Dublin West by-election
2 June	First meeting of group to form Right2Water
9 August	10,000 at Ireland Palestine Solidarity Campaign march against Israel's attack on Gaza
August	Parents for Choice founded
15–24 September	Asylum seeker protest and lockout at Kinsale Road Direct Provision Centre in Cork, more protests follow at other Direct Provision Centres
September	Movement of Asylum Seekers in Ireland (MASI) founded
27–Septenber	5,000 at third annual March for Choice
10 October	Paul Murphy (SP) elected in Dublin South-West by-election
11 October	100,000 at first Right2Water march in Dublin
1 November	150,000–200,000 at second Right2Water demonstrations across the country

	15 November	Labour Party leader and Tánaiste (Deputy Prime Minister) Joan Burton trapped in her car at anti-water charges protest. Arrests later made, including Paul Murphy, TD
	10 December	80,000 at third Right2Water march in Dublin
2015	**26 January**	Syriza government formed in Greece
	9 March	Yes Equality, the pro Marriage Equality campaign group officially launches
	21 March	80,000 at Right2Water march in Dublin
	May	Irish Housing Network established
	22 May	Referendum for Marriage Equality passes 62 per cent to 38 per cent
	12 July	Syriza government forced to sign up to harsh bailout programme
	15 July	Social Democrats launched
	31 October	Right2Change launched
	1 July–14 August	Bolt Hostel – a derelict city council property in Dublin – occupied by activists to house homeless people
	29 August	50,000 at Right2Water march
2016	**23 January**	30 Right2Water demonstrations across the country
	5 February	Anti-Muslim group PEGIDA beaten off the streets of Dublin by counter demonstrators
	20 February	80,000 at Right2Water march
	26 February	General election – Labour decimated. Sinn Féin gains seats. Slight increase for radical left. Fine Gael forms minority government
	April	Need Abortion Ireland established to provide practical support to women seeking abortion
	24 September	25,000 at fifth annual March for Choice
	24 September	Militant republican group Saoradh founded

	25 November	Citizens Assembly on the Eighth Amendment holds first meeting
	15 December 2016– 12 January 2017	Apollo House occupation by Home Sweet Home to protest homelessness and to house homeless people
2017	8 March	Strike for Repeal demonstration
	April	Labour Party cuts ties with unions
	April 23	Citizens' Assembly votes to replace the Eighth Amendment
	15 June	Government announces it will hold a referendum on abortion in 2018
	30 September	30,000–40,000 at sixth annual March for Choice
	30 September	Migrants and Ethnic Minorities for Reproductive Justice is formed
2018	February	SWP changes its name to Socialist Worker Network and announces its focus will be on PBP
	22 March	Public launch of Together for Yes to campaign to repeal the Eighth Amendment
	25 May	Referendum to repeal the Eighth Amendment passes 66 per cent to 34 per cent
	7 August	Take Back the City begins month long series of occupations of empty buildings in Dublin city centre
	3 October	10,000 at Raise the Roof march on the housing crisis
	6 December	Several hundred assemble for far-right anti-immigration protest in Dublin
2019	Spring–summer	Socialist Party split
	28 September	2,000 march against refugees being housed in Oughterard, Co. Galway
	October	Community Action Tenants Union (CATU) formed

2020	**8 February**	General election. Sinn Féin gets more votes than any other party. Fianna Fáil, Fine Gael and Greens form government
	11 March	WHO declares Covid pandemic. Irish schools, universities close down the following day. Lockdown begins

Glossary and Abbreviations

AAA	Anti-Austerity Alliance
ARC	Abortion Rights Campaign. Organisation founded in 2012 to campaign on abortion rights
ATGWU	Amalgamated Transport and General Workers' Union
CAHWT	Campaign Against Household and Water Taxes. Campaigning group against household charges
CATU	Community Action Tenants Union
CPSU	Civil and Public Services Union
CSO	Central Statistics Office
Dáil	Irish house of parliament
DDI	Direct Democracy Ireland
ECB	European Central Bank
Éirígí	Left republican group that split from Sinn Féin in 2006
EU	European Union
FDI	foreign direct investment
Fianna Fáil	centre-right party that was the dominant governing party since independence
Fine Gael	centre right party that was the alternative governing party since independence
Gardaí	Irish police. Singular: garda
Green Party	environmentalist party that served as occasional junior coalition partners with Fianna Fáil and Fine Gael
ICTU	Irish Congress of Trade Unions
IHN	Irish Housing Network
IMF	International Monetary Fund
IRA	Irish Republican Army

Labour	centre-left party that served as occasional junior coalition partners with Fianna Fáil and Fine Gael
MASI	Movement of Asylum Seekers in Ireland
MEP	Member of the European Parliament
NAMA	National Assets Management Agency. State organisation which bailed out insolvent property developers
PBP	People Before Profit. Trotskyist party established by SWP in 2005
Right2Change	Union-supported leftwing campaign platform at the 2016 elections
RIRA	Real Irish Republican Army
Sinn Féin	centre-left and republican 32-county party, formerly the political wing of the IRA
SIPTU	Services, Industrial, Professional and Technical Union. Ireland's largest union
Social Democrats	centre-left party that split from Labour in 2015
SP	Socialist Party. Trotskyist party
SWN	Socialist Workers Network
SWP	Socialist Workers Party. Trotskyist party
TD	Teachta Dála. Irish word for member of parliament
TFY	Together for Yes. Alliance founded in 2018 to campaign on the referendum on abortion
Troika	the group that administered Ireland's austerity programme from 2010 to 2013. It comprised the European Commission, the ECB and the IMF
ULA	United Left Alliance. Electoral alliance between left groups 2011–13
WSM	Workers Solidarity Movement. Anarchist group that disbanded in 2021
WUAG	Tipperary-based Workers and Unemployed Action Group

1

Introduction

Oisín Gilmore and David Landy

When we said to our leftwing friends that we were producing this book on the Irish left during the austerity years, many dryly joked, 'a short book so?' Other responses were along the lines of arguing that the left was useless during those years. When we argued back that no, not only did the left both shift public opinion and have some real victories (a near unique achievement in western Europe during this period), but other countries could learn from these successes, they grudgingly admitted that maybe we weren't completely dire all the time, but still ...

We see these reactions as being more than the expression of a culture of pessimism and instinctive leftwing oppositionalism, including towards itself. They help explain the paradox of the Irish left during this period.

Objectively, we were right. Through its campaigning, the left achieved significant successes, mobilised hundreds of thousands and changed the political culture of Ireland, and this has resulted in a transformed electoral landscape.

The left won important victories on the social and economic front – it stopped the imposition of water charges which would have led to privatisation, and it overthrew the ban on abortion through a mass grassroots campaign. And even when it didn't win – for instance, in the failed campaign against Household Charges or the ongoing campaign for affordable, secure housing – it engaged with people's struggles against austerity in a concrete and sustained way, and mobilised people on a near unprecedented scale.

For a country that had little history of mass demonstration, it was normal for there to be multiple demonstrations every year with over 10,000 people in Dublin, a city of 1.2 million. Nearly every year between 2009 and 2016 there was at least one demonstration with more than 80,000 people. This is the equivalent of yearly demonstrations of well over half a million in London or Paris. In the early years these were normally trade union demonstrations, while in the later years they were mainly against the water tax. Tens of thousands participated in this movement against the water tax, with two-thirds of households actively refusing to pay the tax. And the movement for the repeal of the Eighth Amendment of the constitution, which banned abortion, while not directly connected to the question of austerity, yet fuelled by heightened political awareness, saw the largest feminist movement in the history of the country develop and achieve the legalisation of abortion in the Republic.

Electorally, the left was rewarded for this engagement, Trotskyist parties and Sinn Féin, the leftwing republican party, both secured impressive and unprecedented victories at local elections in 2014 and general elections in 2011 and 2016. This theme of unprecedented victories is important. Unlike other European countries with strong leftwing traditions, and even leftwing governments, Ireland has been dominated by centre-right parties since the south became independent in 1922. However, in the 2011 election, the leading party, Fianna Fáil, collapsed, and for the first time ever a social democratic party, the Labour Party, became the second largest party. Sinn Féin went from winning four out of 158 seats in the Dáil (the state parliament) before the crisis to 23 in 2016, and 37 in 2020. And the two Trotskyist parties have had what is perhaps the most electoral success in the history of western Trotskyism, winning six seats in the Dáil in 2016.

So why the long faces on the left? Why the assumption of failure? This is partly because when we started this project in late 2019, before the pandemic, it was becoming clear that despite all the remarkable movements between 2008 and 2018, this wave of struggle had definitely subsided.

Any enthusiasm from the impressive electoral performance of Labour in 2011 rapidly dissipated after they entered government and implemented the austerity agenda. Sinn Féin won only 81 seats in the 2019 local elections against its 159 in 2014, and the two Trotskyist groups won only eleven against their previous 28. And these organisations also faced significant internal problems.

Outside of electoral politics, the Repeal movement, while still widely felt, had largely dissipated, having almost entirely achieved its aim. Likewise with the water tax – while many key activists from the water charges movement progressed onto campaigning on housing, this campaign hasn't gained nearly the same amount of traction or public support.

Since 2019, Sinn Féin recovered electorally and is now poised for government, but other leftwing parties and campaigns have struggled in the face of the new political challenges, which the far right have been more able to take advantage of. As we discuss in the conclusion, Chapter 11, while the recent Palestine solidarity movement demonstrates the left's continued ability to mobilise large numbers, and the growth of Sinn Féin and the Trotskyist party, People Before Profit, demonstrate a widespread support for leftwing politics, the left has failed to build lasting political and social institutions. Despite their electoral success, left parties remain small and are highly dependent on their elected representatives. And there is a lack of physical spaces, media platforms and social and cultural institutions in which leftwing people can assemble, discuss and draw others in. After a decade that saw the left win real victories, mobilise hundreds of thousands and transform the electoral landscape, in many ways the left finds itself in a strangely weak position.

This book's central conversation is about this paradox. It is a contradiction wherein the left was able to win major victories but faces an uncertain future. We think that both sides of this coin are important – it is important to understand both how the left was able to influence the course of events and what the limits are to this success.

HISTORICAL BACKGROUND

Irish people love to talk about how Ireland is not a normal country. Of course, no country is normal. But such delight in perversity does point to something true: the fact that Ireland, with its colonial history, is indeed unusual in western European politics. Related to this, it is the only democracy in western Europe where a socialist or social democratic party has never led a government. The recent progress of the left in Ireland, growing from a weak position to a relatively strong one, stands in stark contrast with the rest of western Europe, where in nearly every country the left has gone from strength to weakness, winning almost no victories and suffering continuous electoral decline.

Understanding the development of the left in Ireland, therefore, requires some understanding of Irish history and of how, with its colonial history, it differs from other western European states. This introduction aims to provide a historical background for the chapters that follow – firstly, giving an overview of how Ireland's struggle with colonialism has affected contemporary politics, then turning to the 2008 crisis and how the left responded. In this way, we introduce the chapters and the logic of the book – exploring both the movements of the last decade and the political groups behind them, from anarchists and Trotskyists to republicans and social democrats.

Ireland's Colonial Experience and the Struggle Against It

If, in twentieth-century western Europe, politics was dominated by the challenge to capitalism posed by the socialist labour movement, then the dominant question of Irish politics, like other colonial and post-colonial states, was the relationship with the former colonial master. This continued well after the wars in the early twentieth century that won partial independence for the southern 26 counties of Ireland. This question was the main political divide between the two leading parties in the south. Cumann na nGaedheal (which later became Fine Gael) advocated maintaining the economic ties with England that defined pre-independence Ireland. In contrast, Fianna Fáil advocated a new independent path of economic development.

England's colonisation of Ireland between 1550 and 1700 had sought to replace the indigenous Catholic population with Protestant 'settlers', so that already by the late 1650s Catholic ownership of land had collapsed to just 14 per cent, concentrated in the western province of Connacht.[1] This loss of property was followed by a set of 'Penal Laws', which excluded Catholics from almost all spheres of public life.

The decades that followed saw the emergence of a new Anglo-Irish ruling class loyal to the British crown. But, by the late eighteenth century, this class was calling for greater legislative autonomy from Britain. However, they faced a problem in that the vast majority of the population in Ireland was Catholic and landless, while the governing class were a small minority of landed Protestants. To what extent should Catholics be allowed to participate in the political and public life of Ireland was a debate that raged in late eighteenth-century Ireland.

The next century and a half of Irish politics was dominated by the question of whether Irish freedom would mean the maintenance of existing property relations with allowance made for the incorporation of Catholics into the elite, or the transformation of property relations through the democratisation of the country.

The connected question of property rights and republican democracy can be seen clearly in the Proclamation of the Irish Republic issued by the Irish Republican Brotherhood (also known as the Fenians) in their abortive rising of 1867. It stated:

All men are born with equal rights, and in associating together to protect one another and share public burdens, justice demands that such associations should rest upon a basis which maintains equality instead of destroying it. … [W]e aim at founding a Republic based on universal suffrage, which shall secure to all the intrinsic value of their labour.

And it ended with an appeal to the working class of England:

As for you, workmen of England, it is not only your hearts we wish, but your arms. Remember the starvation and degradation brought to your firesides by the oppression of labour. Remember the past, look well to the future, and avenge yourselves by giving liberty to your children in the coming struggle for human freedom. Herewith we proclaim the Irish Republic.

While often portrayed as simply a national conflict between England and Ireland, the struggle for an Irish republic was an entangled struggle for popular democracy and transformed property relations. The revolutionary period at the start of the twentieth century brought together agrarian struggles against landlordism, revolutionary syndicalism and a revived national identity in the fight for an Irish republic. In 1916 an insurrection led by the Irish Republican Brotherhood and the socialist Irish Citizen Army declared an Irish republic.

While the 1916 rebellion was quickly crushed, republicans organising themselves in the Sinn Féin party won the 1918 election. They refused to take their seats in the UK House of Commons and formed a parliament in Dublin loyal to the republic declared in 1916. When the first meeting of this parliament (the Dáil) met in January 1919, they committed the republic to a 'Democratic Programme' which opened by stating:

> we declare that the Nation's sovereignty extends not only to all men and women of the Nation, but to all its material possessions, the Nation's soil and all its resources, all the wealth and all the wealth-producing processes within the Nation, and ... we reaffirm that all right to private property must be subordinated to the public right and welfare.

Simultaneous with the revolutionary republican movement of 1916–23, the labour movement exploded. While in 1915 there were 152,000 strike days, by 1920 this had increased to 1,447,000.[2] Between 1919 and 1923 a series of so called 'soviets' were declared when workers seized control of their workplaces. For two weeks in 1919, a 'soviet' even controlled the city of Limerick.

A guerilla war between the Irish Republican Army (IRA), which was loyal to the republic of 1916 and the Dáil of 1919, and the British forces was fought between 1919 and 1921. However, the subsequent treaty signed between the IRA's negotiators and the British government fell far short of a full republic. The island was partitioned along sectarian lines, with a Protestant-dominated state in the north loyal to the British Empire, and a Catholic-dominated state in the south. Both states would be allowed self-government, although both would remain part of the British Empire.

For those who understood Irish freedom as meaning the incorporation of Irish Catholics into the social elite, the treaty achieved this in the south. But for those who understood Irish freedom to mean the democratisation of the country with the resulting transformation of property relations, the treaty closed off these hopes. The treaty firmly locked Ireland into the British imperial order, both politically and economically.

The signing of the treaty led to a civil war which pitted those who wanted to fight for an independent republic of the entire country against those who believed that a limited Catholic state in the south was the most they could (or, in some cases, wished to) achieve. The republicans lost and the victors formed a new party, Cumann na nGaedheal, which went on to take power over the southern state in Ireland. This state was initially named the Irish Free State, but from 1937 it took the name 'Ireland'. (The rest of this book is primarily focused on the southern state, and the book uses the state's name 'Ireland' despite the fact that the southern state does not cover the entire island of Ireland. This terminological issue is discussed later in this chapter.)

After 'Independence': From Neo-colony to Celtic Tiger

The new Cumann na nGaedheal government was both socially and economically conservative. Some power was transferred to a domestic Catholic elite, who benefited from and continued to maintain Ireland's subservient relation with the British economy. As the historian Conor McCabe writes, Ireland's 'role was to provide agricultural produce for the industrial centres of Britain, and this was done mainly in the form of live cattle exports'.[3] Alongside this economic dependency on Britain, there was a growing spiritual and cultural dependency on Rome – the influence of the Catholic church on all areas of life intensified following independence.

Following its defeat in the civil war, the republican movement split in 1926. Much of the leadership of the remaining IRA were committed socialists, and the question of their relationship with the international communist movement proved a controversial issue in the years that followed. However, the larger organisation that emerged from this split in the republican movement was Fianna Fáil, which decided to make peace with the Irish Free State and work within its institutions. Fianna Fáil quickly rose to power and went on to dominate the politics of the southern state from its election to government in 1932 to the 2011 election during the Great Recession.

By the time Fianna Fáil was elected to government in 1932, Ireland was 'virtually the last predominantly free-trading economy in the world'.[4] The Fianna Fáil government, however, pursued a different policy of increased economic self-reliance, with the introduction of protection, the promotion of tillage for domestic consumption over pasture for export, promoting the breaking up of large farms, some redistribution of land, as well as defaulting on annuities owed to Britain, and pursuing the development of domestic manufacturing.[5]

The standard narrative of this period is that Fianna Fáil introduced protection, which massively damaged the Irish economy. This was only corrected when the liberal hero, the civil servant T. K. Whitaker took over the Department of Finance in 1956 and developed the liberal free-trade policies that led to the Celtic Tiger. There are a number of problems with the story. Firstly, the economy did not significantly underperform in the 1930s or 1940s and was not unusually protectionist.[6] Secondly, the economy did not take off after Whitaker. In fact, while the economy did not perform much worse than its neighbours in the 1930s or 1940s, it did perform much worse between the 1950s and 1980s.

That is not to say that there were no significant changes to economic policy in the 1950s. New government agencies were founded to develop the Irish exporting sector. This export-oriented industrialisation strategy, with a key role for foreign direct investment, ultimately laid the foundations of the Celtic Tiger at the end of the twentieth century. Initial success was marked by gross domestic product (GDP) growth rates of on average 3.7 per cent between 1960 and 1973. These were high for Ireland but low relatively to other western European countries.

A challenge was that through this period Ireland remained completely tied with the British economy, which underperformed in the post-war period. Ireland's future strategy of being a low-cost base for US multinationals in Europe was therefore closed off in the post-war period. All that Ireland had to offer was that it could be a low-cost base into the sluggish British economy. With the entry of the UK and Ireland into the European Economic Community in 1973, the offer became much more appealing. Income levels converged towards those of the UK during the seventies, and, relative to France, they stabilised after declining for the previous three decades.[7]

The subsequent decade of the 1980s was a period of poor economic performance in many countries. But, in Ireland, this was arguably the worst period since independence. In the late 1970s and early 1980s, successive governments responded to the impact of high oil prices and a poor global economy with deficit spending. This drove the Irish debt below 60 per cent of GNP in the mid-1970s to over 115 per cent by 1988.[8] Due to high interest rates, this drove the share of GNP accounted for by debt interest payment to a shocking peak in 1985 of 10 per cent of GNP![9] This deficit spending was highly ineffective, and, between 1979 and 1986, private consumption barely rose, but unemployment rose from 6.8 per cent to 17.1 per cent, the highest level in the history of the state.

However, the period after 1987 marked a notable change in Irish economic fortunes. Government spending contracted sharply, and debt came down. Tied to this was the start of a programme of 'social partnership', where unions, employers and government would agree three-year economic development programmes. With access to the European economy, a young, English-speaking, educated workforce and a low-cost, pro-business environment, Ireland became an attractive place for foreign multinationals to set up base and sell into Europe. Between 1990 and 2003, growth per annum averaged 6.4 per cent, and Ireland went from being a poor peripheral economy to having one of the highest per capita national income figures in the world.

After many years of Ireland being a backward economy, it felt like the country had arrived. And lessons were learned from Ireland's experience. Central to the economic take-off had been American investment, European economic integration, free-trade policies, low business taxation, a highly educated workforce and a labour movement muzzled by social partnership. And this was reflected in popular politics. The political climate created by this economic boom was a solidly centre-right one, with nearly universal support for neoliberal politics. There was little interest or appetite for leftwing politics based on labour militancy, state intervention in the economy, or any kind of turning away from US investment or the European Union (EU) market.

Politically dominated by the centre right, Ireland was a country that had leap-frogged from a primarily agricultural economy to a high-tech economy, with a workforce concentrated in services and advanced manufacturing. The absence of a large industrial working class and the fact that Ireland was a post-colonial society meant that politics in Ireland was atypical of a western European country. The socialist labour movement was always a minority. Despite one or two good elections,[10] between 1923 and 1992 support for the Labour Party rarely rose above 10 per cent. Rather, left political ambitions were generally pursued through Irish republicanism, either through the politically dominant Fianna Fáil, or through smaller groups such as Clann na Poblachta, Sinn Féin or the IRA.

In the early 1990s, however, there were some signs of a growing support for leftwing politics on social issues. Ireland was still dominated by the Catholic church, and deference to the church's teaching on sexuality was widespread and institutionalised, with divorce and abortion still illegal, and homosexuality a crime. The gap on these issues and more generally on women's rights and minority rights between Ireland and other European countries was at this stage very stark.

This slight shift to the left could be seen in the election of the feminist lawyer Mary Robinson as president in 1990, the Labour Party doubling its vote in 1992 and the tens of thousands that came out to protest against restrictive abortion laws in the same year. (See Chapter 4.) Electorally, the combined support for left parties increased from its 1970s–1980s level of 12–15 per cent to around 20–25 per cent, where it remained for the next 20 years. Major concerns for the left during this period were poverty reduction and social issues such as divorce, gay rights and women's rights.

But the left remained weak and marginal throughout this period. The percentage of votes going to rightwing parties was 3.8 times as much as those going to leftwing parties in the 1997 election and remained 3.1 times as much in both the 2003 and 2007 elections.[11]

Such was the calm before the storm. Shortly after the 2007 election, the 2008 financial crisis erupted. The resulting economic crisis and the struggles in response to it transformed Ireland.

The End of the Celtic Tiger

The story of the Celtic Tiger was in many ways a simple one. After decades of lagging behind its western European neighbours, between 1990 and 2000 the Irish economy caught up with them. However, this kind of catch-up growth is a story with an end. If an economy with low levels of productivity manages to increase its productivity until it catches up with high productivity economies, once that has happened, elevated levels of catch-up growth should subside. However, in the case of Ireland between 2000 and 2007, despite converging on high productivity economies, high levels of growth continued on the basis of a credit-fuelled housing bubble.[12]

While European integration had been a key ingredient for Irish economic success, in the late 1990s and early 2000s Ireland was at a different point in the business cycle than most of the other members of the Eurozone. While in Ireland the economy was booming and experiencing full employment, many other European countries, such as Germany, were experiencing high levels of unemployment. This imbalance within the Eurozone created a problem.

Ireland's low unemployment and high growth created the possibility of the economy 'overheating' with growing inflation and rising asset prices. A state with its own monetary policy would normally respond to that by increasing interest rates. However, as Ireland was part of the Eurozone, interest rates in Ireland were set in Frankfurt, which kept interest rates low in order to deal with persistently high unemployment in core EU member states.

Low interest rates, elevated levels of domestic demand and a flow of cheap capital from the Eurozone core economies led to property bubbles developing across several European economies, including Ireland. This was not helped by the fact that the Irish government did little to address the overheating of the Irish economy. On the contrary, the governing party, Fianna Fáil, had close links with property developers and it facilitated and even encouraged a speculative property boom. Irish banks also leaned into the boom, borrowing excessively, lending recklessly and ultimately in a number of cases becoming insolvent.

When the global property bubble burst and the credit crunch hit in 2008, Ireland was very exposed. Operating under the mistaken

belief that Irish banks merely faced temporary liquidity con-
straints, the Minister for Finance provided a broad government
guarantee of the liabilities of Irish banks in September 2008. This
'bank guarantee' ultimately led to a 'bank bailout' as it became
clear that a number of Irish banks were not simply facing a temporary liquidity crisis but were insolvent. All but one of the six main
Irish banks were nationalised, and billions were pumped into these
banks to recapitalise them and cover their losses.[13] In total, over
€60 billion were poured into the failing Irish banks. For comparison, annual gross national income between 2009 and 2012 was
around €140 billion.[14]

The collapse of the property market had a major impact on
government tax revenue, while the dramatic increase in unemployment put further pressure on the state finances. Over the
subsequent two years the fiscal impact of the bank bailout became
clearer and, by the second half of 2010, the state was running
massive deficits and debt was spiralling out of control. In 2007, the
debt to GDP ratio was only 25 per cent, in just three years that had
risen to 95 per cent.[15]

The government turned to the International Monetary Fund
(IMF) and EU for a bailout, and, in November 2010, a bailout
agreement was agreed with the 'Troika': the IMF, the European
Commission and the European Central Bank (ECB). The €85
billion Economic Adjustment programme involved €67.5 billion
from external sources (€45 billion from the EU and EU member
states, and €22.5 billion from the IMF) and a further €17.5 billion
was raided from Ireland's National Pension Reserve Fund.

Savage cuts in public spending were also made while taxes
were increased. The austerity measures introduced between 2008
and 2010, before the EU-IMF programme, already amounted to
€14 billion, and, under the EU-IMF programme, further austerity measures of €15 billion were planned for between 2011 and
2014.[16] The cumulative €29 billion austerity measures amounted
to around 20 per cent of national income!

While it was the wealthy who had gained the most from the
boom years and property bubble of the early 2000s, it was the least
well off who suffered most during these years. One in seven jobs
were lost, construction and retail being hardest hit, with unem-

ployment for young people skyrocketing from 8 per cent in 2007 to 33 per cent in 2012.[17] Those with jobs suffered tax increases and cuts in pay in both private and public sectors, with more low-paid workers brought into the tax net. While one-third of the austerity measures were covered through tax increases and new measures such as the household tax and universal service charge, two-thirds were the result of spending cuts. Social welfare, education and health were hardest hit. Support payments such as maternity benefit and child benefit were cut, as were services across the board. Health spending was cut by 27 per cent between 2009 and 2014.[18] This created a collapse in living standards, experienced by many – 31 per cent of the population in 2010 reported that it was 'difficult' or 'very difficult' to live on their household income[19] – but especially suffered by those on low incomes dependent on state supports. All the indications of poverty – homelessness, hunger, material deprivation – soared during the austerity years. In response, an estimated 265,000 Irish citizens left the country to find work elsewhere between 2009 and 2015. Over 70 per cent of these were aged in their twenties.[20] This in a state with a population of only 4.5 million, of whom in 2009 only 755,000 were aged in their twenties.[21] The Central Statistics Office (CSO) estimates that 83,000 emigrated in 2012 alone. This exceeds even the highest rates of emigration in the past, such as in the 1950s and 1980s.[22]

The shock of the economic crisis was sudden, but economic recovery also began relatively quickly. Already by 2009, real GDP, exports and domestic demand were increasing. However, unemployment took longer to recover. Unemployment continued to increase until 2012, when it peaked at 15.9 per cent, before gradually declining to 4.8 per cent in late 2019.[23] Likewise, the total number employed in the economy did not reach the 2007 high of 2.25 million until 2018. Today there are 2.7 million in employment.

Despite this economic recovery, ordinary workers in Ireland are struggling. If we look at Actual Individual Consumption, a national income measure that captures both what is directly spent by households and what is spent on both market and non-market consumption goods by non-profits and government (for example, on primary education), and adjusts for purchasing power, Irish households have not recovered from the drop in their consumption arising from the economic crisis. In 2007, Irish households had consumption levels comparable to France or Germany, today they are significantly lower.[24]

A myth sometimes told about the Irish recovery is that it demonstrates that the EU-IMF medicine can work. It is worth stating that this is false in almost every sense. A problem faced by the EU-IMF programme in Ireland was that there was little they could do to 'reform' the Irish economy. There was relatively little that could be privatised that had not already been privatised, and few labour rights or trade union powers that could be undermined. Ireland was already the perfect neoliberal society before the EU and IMF arrived. While the EU-IMF package required austerity and major cuts to public spending, it did not require many major reforms. One of the only significant reforms the programme required was the introduction of water charges, and as Chapter 3 shows, the attempt to do so proved a total disaster for the government. What really drove Ireland's recovery were the exports of Irish-based US multinationals. Therefore, recovering demand in the global markets mattered far more than anything else.

THE RESPONSE TO AUSTERITY AND
THE STRUCTURE OF THIS BOOK

Austerity in Ireland was severe and widely felt. But as the government cut, ordinary people reacted, and there was a wave of social movements between 2008 and 2013. The country did not simply experience an economic crisis but a crisis of legitimacy during these years. The government had bet the house on a failed economic gamble, and there was widespread shock and anger among Irish people – not simply at the scale of their suffering – but the incompetence of the governing class that had led to it. The early movements were focused on the most egregious of the austerity measures – hospital closures, pension cuts, cuts in pay and the household tax, which was seen as a form of poll tax. These movements initially looked to the trade unions and the Labour Party to lead the fight against austerity – but as these institutions began administering and accommodating austerity, as David Landy in Chapter 2 recounts, leadership in combatting austerity passed to more radical leftwing groups. However, these groups initially didn't seem to succeed in harnessing the widespread public anger at the cuts and other austerity measures, and appeared to achieve little.

The major change in the early years came at the ballot box. The electoral response to the crisis was sharp. Fianna Fáil, which had been the dominant party in Irish politics since 1932, was decimated in the 2011 election called shortly after the 2010 EU-IMF bailout was agreed. In 2007 Fianna Fáil won 77 seats. In 2011 it won only 20. While much of that vote simply went to Fine Gael, the other centre-right party, there was also a significant swing to the left. The Labour Party more than doubled its vote from 209,000 to 431,000 and increased its vote share from 10.1 per cent to 19.4 per cent. While in 2007 more than three times as many people voted for a right party than left party, by 2011 that had dropped to 1.5 times as many.[25]

In some ways, the 2011 election took the wind out of the sails of the early anti-austerity movement. This movement had been led by the trade union movement, which was largely aligned with the Labour Party. After Labour went into government in 2011, the trade union movement took a much more quiescent role. Chapter 6 on the trade union movement discusses the difficult place that unions, weakened from years of partnership and falling union density found themselves in. After some early stirrings of militancy, unions reverted to a pattern of concessions and bargaining with government. They felt they had little choice, especially during the Troika years when the government showed itself more than willing to run roughshod over union concerns and working conditions. With the return to a measure of economic independence and recovery after 2013, unions managed to win some small victories but still found themselves in a weak position. However, as Mary Muldowney points out in the chapter, their adoption of an organising over a services model offers some hopes for the future.

As for the other pillar of social democracy, the Labour Party, it abandoned its pre-election commitment to pursue a different path to that laid out in the EU-IMF programme. As they implemented austerity their support collapsed, with some members splitting and setting up the Social Democrats, a party with little programmatic difference to the Labour Party but free of the taint of the 2011–16 government. The story of the rise, fall and fracturing of the Labour Party is given in Chapter 7 by Paul Dillon.

After the 2011 election, the anti-austerity movement only really recovered when the government attempted to introduce charges for domestic water consumption, with the inevitable long-run outcome of water privatisation. The movement against the water charges exploded in late 2014 with a series of massive marches and widespread civil disobedience. Over two-thirds of households refused to pay the tax and tens of thousands actively participated in the movement against it. This story of how an unwieldly coalition of left parties, trade unions and community groups managed to come together to defeat the water charges and then sought to build on this victory through an electoral alliance is told by Dave Gibney, in Chapter 3.

While support for the Labour Party collapsed in the 2014 local elections and the 2016 general election, support for the left did not. Sinn Féin replaced Labour as the largest party on the left, and smaller radical left parties performed remarkably well. The two Trotskyist groups, the Socialist Workers Party (SWP) and the Socialist Party, had both played major roles in anti-austerity campaigning. Their wider electoral vehicles – respectively People Before Profit and the Anti-Austerity Alliance – won 14 seats each in the 2014 local elections and, after forming an electoral alliance in 2015, won a combined six Dáil seats in the 2016 general election. A further three independent socialist TDs were also of Trotskyist lineage.[26] This means that more than one in 20 members of the parliament was a Trotskyist.

The story of leftwing groups wasn't one of unalloyed success though. While the SWP successfully turned People Before Profit into an ongoing feature of the Irish political landscape, the Socialist Party split and collapsed. David Landy, in Chapter 9, recounts the differing fortunes of these groups and examines the fortunes of one of the major what-might-have-been of these years – the ill-fated United Left Alliance.

Nor was it clean sailing for republican groups. Chapter 10 looks at the fortunes of republicanism during austerity. Dan Finn casts an eye on Sinn Féin's bumpy rise during the decade – observing how they tacked both left and right in an effort to find a formula that would appeal to the public and prove that they were fit for government. Their success – in 2020 they won the most votes of any political party even though they were still excluded from government – stands in contrast to more militant republican groups. Stewart Reddin and Damian Lawlor in the same chapter examine the failure of Éirígí, the main republican group to the left of Sinn Féin during this period, despite its active opposition to austerity and its reaching out to other groups on the left.

Another failure was the collapse of anarchism in Ireland. At the start of the recession, the Workers Solidarity Movement was a long-standing, well-known and very active anarchist group. Its implosion during the decade is a salutary tale of burn-out and bust, told by Kevin Doyle in Chapter 8.

Despite the changing fortunes experienced by political groups, there was growing confidence among the left that victories could be won. After the 2016 election and because of the mass campaign against water charges, the plans for their introduction were dropped in 2016. This marked a late but real and substantial victory for the anti-austerity movement. This built a sense that popular struggle can win victories. And, building also on the experience of the successful 2015 gay marriage referendum, the pro-choice movement, which had been growing since 2012, successfully forced the government to call a referendum in 2018 to legalise abortion. This movement grew into what was almost certainly the largest feminist movement in the history of the state, and one of the largest feminist movements in the western world in recent decades. Thousands upon thousands canvassed and campaigned before and after the 2018 referendum, which was ultimately won with a two-thirds majority. Aillen O'Carroll and Máire Ni Chuagáin discuss the antecedents to this victory and how the Abortion Rights Campaign organised, fought and won the fight for reproductive rights.

It was after the victory of this campaign that we began the project that led to this book. At the time there was a widespread questioning of what was next for the left. But by 2019, it was becoming clear that there was no significant movement on the horizon. It was not clear how the left might build on its previous success.

In the 2019 local elections, while the vote for the left remained similar to 2014, the impact in terms of seats was devastating, with Sinn Féin losing nearly half its seats and the Trotskyists losing 17 of their 28 seats.

The one social movement growing during this period was the housing movement. This was in response to a growing housing crisis. The CSO reports that between 2012 and 2023, the average house price in Ireland more than doubled, from €155,114 to €333,259; in Dublin, it increased from €240,333 to €477,129.[27] Increases have not been restricted to house price increases. Rents have also doubled. The standardised average rent in new tenancies was stable at around €800 per month from 2009 to 2015. By late 2023 it had doubled to €1,600 per month.[28] Needless to say, wages had not seen any kind of similar increase. Between 2008 and 2016 average weekly earnings were fairly stable at around €700. By late 2023 they increased to around €900.[29] However, housing is a more difficult issue to campaign on than, say, water charges or abortion – complex issues, but ones with clear demands and targets. The story of the housing movement is told in Chapter 5 – in particular the 'movement from below' and the development of direct action, which has led to the growth of the Community Action Tenants Union (CATU), an ongoing campaign to organise for housing rights.

In the 2020 election, Sinn Féin swung to the left and campaigned on housing. It committed to an unprecedented housebuilding programme, saying it would build 100,000 public homes on public land.[30] And it was rewarded for it. In a surprise result, it won 24.5 per cent of the vote, a larger share than any other party, and nearly every single candidate it stood in the election was elected.[31] The combined vote for all right parties was only marginally above the combined vote for left parties.

From the summer of 2021 until the summer of 2024, support for the left was in most polls higher than support for the right. However, in the run up to the local and European elections of June 2024, there was an increase in support for independents and small far-right anti-immigrant parties. This topic is discussed in the conclusion, Chapter 11.

THE APPROACH OF THIS BOOK

This book is the end product of a collective project to examine the victories and defeats of the Irish left since 2008, systematically examining the main components of left movements in order to come to an understanding of these years of struggle. The project began in late 2019, and involved a series of public discussion meetings, which were unfortunately cut short by the COVID-19 lockdown in 2020.

The approach taken in this project has been to try to approach the Irish left with open eyes. We do not believe that the road to a post-capitalist future is already mapped out for us in some text by some guru either from the past or the present. There are things to learn from every socialist tradition, but we cannot rely on only studying heroic days from a century ago. It is by studying the struggles, conflicts and possibilities of our present and our recent past that we can work out where we stand and, from there, where we might advance in the future.

Indeed, we have been campaigning for social and economic justice in Ireland for decades and in that time have seen dynamic and important movements and campaigns being consigned to the dustbin of memory once they ran their courses, their lessons often only half-learned – if at all. It's vital that this is not the fate of movements and campaigns of the recession years.

While some of the authors of chapters in this book work in academia, this is not intended to be a book by and for academics. The chapters are all written by activists involved in or adjacent to the movements they're writing about, and the purpose of each chapter is to critically yet sympathetically analyse each major campaign and group on the Irish left. We encourage readers to read the author bios before reading each chapter.

As some of our critics predicted, it's a short book, and as such we had to leave some movements out. The main groups and movements we didn't give a chapter to were those on anti-racism and migrant rights, LGBT+ rights, environmentalism and international solidarity. All these movements could conceivably have had a chapter. Migrants organised in this period through the Anti-Racism Network and the Movement of Asylum Seekers in Ireland

(MASI), the latter winning an important victory in getting the government to agree to abolish Direct Provision in 2020 – though since then the situation has only gotten worse for asylum seekers. However, regrettably, these movements were on the periphery of the Irish left and mostly sidelined in this period, only moving into more central focus in recent years. As Chapter 5 discusses, migrant inclusion in the housing movement was not a given, but rather a hard-fought victory. In like manner, anti-fascism has long been an aspect of the Irish left – but as a large-scale far right has only arisen in reaction to the loss of the abortion referendum and flourished under the strains of Brexit and the COVID-19 pandemic, this now central issue in leftwing politics lies outside the scope of the book, but is addressed in the conclusion.

The LGBT+ movement of course won a major victory when the Marriage Equality referendum passed in May 2015 by a majority of 62 per cent of voters. That this was celebrated by rightwing liberals, and that a 'yes' vote was supported by all parties – and the heads of many businesses, as well as trade unions – does not make it any less of a leftwing victory. Such a referendum would have been inconceivable 20 years previously, and it is testament to the success of the LGBT+ movement in reversing stigmatised identities and mainstreaming previously fringe political projects that so many came on board. Nevertheless, for most of the left, as opposed to those within the campaign, it was only a brief moment of struggle, lasting at most the few months of the referendum campaign, and more commonly a few weeks. This stands in contrast to the Repeal movement, which was a cornerstone leftwing project for many years.

The struggle for trans rights, or rather against the backlash to these rights – a progressive Gender Recognition Act was passed with no fanfare in 2015 – is longer lasting. However, this struggle is outside the scope of the book as it only really acquired its central importance with the rise of the far right during the pandemic. As recently as 2019, people were still talking about keeping British transphobia out of Irish politics, unsuccessfully as it turned out.

Probably the most depressing omission in this book is that of environmentalism. We couldn't justify including the Green Party. While in government from 2007 to 2011, the party was an enthusiastic imposer of austerity measures. Even after their rejection by the electorate, they continued to justify these regressive measures, as well as supporting new ones. For instance, they were the only opposition party to support the imposition of water charges, which they did on spurious environmental grounds. While there was a small leftwing element in the Green Party, this wasn't hugely active over this period.

A significant example of the regressive nature of the Green Party was their antagonism towards the one environmental campaign of major significance for both the left and the country, the Shell to Sea campaign against Shell's dangerous high-pressure pipeline to process offshore natural gas in the west of Ireland.[32] While the campaign's heyday was in 2005–8 and lies mostly outside our timeline, it is difficult to overestimate its importance for the Irish left. It provided hugely important education to a generation of activists, not just on state and media tactics, but on forms of direct action which they would use later on, especially in the water charges campaign. But beyond Shell to Sea, environmental campaigning remained small-scale, although there was an uptick in activism around climate change towards the end of our period.

We also leave out international solidarity, which remained important in this time, in particular Palestinian solidarity, although there have also been other solidarity campaigns, such as the Greek solidarity campaign, Rojava solidarity and anti-war activism. These were all significant in providing inspiration for the Irish left, but prior to 2023, when a large Palestine solidarity movement emerged in response to Israel's genocide against the people of Gaza, international solidarity movements played a relatively small role in the Irish left during the austerity years.

A final issue is that of partition. Before the partition of Ireland in 1922, the term 'Ireland' was relatively uncomplicated, and it simply referred to the island and the people who lived on it. But after partition, the term itself became a site of political contestation. The southern state, despite being named 'Ireland', clearly does not include all of Ireland.

While we could use alternative terms such as 'the 26 counties', 'Southern Ireland', 'the Republic of Ireland', and so on, these all have issues and can be rather cumbersome. Therefore, the authors in this book generally follow the conventional practice of using the southern state's name for itself, 'Ireland', and throughout this book the terms 'Ireland' and 'Irish' are used to refer to the southern state in Ireland, even though we are aware that using the terms 'Ireland' and 'Irish' to refer to only part of Ireland is highly anachronistic and we reject any partitionist implication their use might suggest.

But, it is the politics of the southern state that is the focus of this book. Although there is some discussion of politics in the northern state in, for example, the chapters on abortion and, of course, republicanism, we mostly focused on the 26 counties of the Republic of Ireland, excluding the six counties of Northern Ireland. This may be disconcerting for an international readership accustomed to viewing Ireland through the lens of the Troubles, the republican struggle against both British occupation and unionist domination of the north of Ireland. But unfortunately, this exclusion of Northern Ireland has a certain logic. Politics, after all, is organised around the state – for instance, all the campaigns on austerity, whether on pay cuts or against the household tax or water charges, were exclusively centred on the southern state. One reason the book focuses on the southern state is because much of the campaigning in question did so too.

We also take this focus because the immediate political context of the north and south was so radically different. In the Republic, weak, centrist governments, amenable to some degree of public pressure, but beholden to an externally imposed austerity programme, were in charge of a collapsed economy. This created the political opportunities for social movements and oppositional consciousness to flourish. In the north, on the other hand, local politics revolved around a Northern Ireland Assembly deadlocked between joint republican and unionist control and unable to engage in any form of meaningful politics – indeed, unable to sit from 2017 to 2020. Real power lay in the aloof, rightwing, British (or more correctly, English) government impervious to Irish concerns. So, although the north was also affected by the recession, austerity hit it in different ways, with less democratic avenues of reaction available to it. Equally important were the different political events facing both parts of Ireland. In Northern Ireland, the constitutional question, which never went away, was given fresh impetus by the

2014 Scottish independence referendum, Brexit and the inexorable march to an Irish nationalist voting majority. These events were far more peripheral to the south. Northern Ireland, in other words, doesn't need another chapter, it needs another book. At the same time, it would be absurd to take a purely partitionist viewpoint, if only because the left didn't in how they organised. Some unions organised both north and south, as did republicans, Trotskyists and anarchists. Though campaigns tended to be confined to political jurisdictions, important overlaps and cooperation took place, such as in the abortion referendum. These connections are highlighted in the relevant chapters.

This book is not an attempt to give a complete or encyclopaedic account of the left in Ireland over recent years. It is not intended to give an accurate representation of the entire left. Rather the book looks at both the largest movements since 2008 and the main components of the Irish left during this period. The former is presented in first part of the book, while the latter is presented in the second part.

This book is not a work of disinterested analysis making spurious claims to objectivity, it is a project with a partisan interest in the struggle for a better future. It is a work of recollection, deliberation, debate, provocation and analysis. We hope that it might play some small part in the development of the Irish left's understanding of itself and of Ireland – its past and its future.

NOTES

1. Micheál Ó Siochrú and David Brown, 'The Down Survey and the Cromwellian Land Settlement', in Jane Ohlmeyer (ed.), *The Cambridge History of Ireland, vol. 2, 1550–1730* (Cambridge: Cambridge University Press, 2018), p. 584.
2. Emmet O'Connor, *Syndicalism in Ireland, 1917–1923* (Cork: Cork University Press, 1988), p. 25.
3. Conor McCabe, *Sins of the Father: The Decisions That Shaped the Irish Economy*, 2nd edition (Dublin: History Press, 2013), p. 61.
4. Peter Neary and Cormac Ó. Gráda, 'Protection, Economic War and Structural Change: The 1930s in Ireland', *Irish Historical Studies* 27, no. 107 (1991): 254.
5. Much of this chapter's discussion of the economic development of Ireland in the twentieth century draws on the work of Cormac Ó Gráda

and Kevin O'Rourke. See in particular: Cormac Ó Gráda and Kevin Hjortshøj O'Rourke, 'The Irish Economy during the Century after Partition', *The Economic History Review* 75, no. 2 (2022): 336–70; Kevin Hjortshøj O'Rourke, 'Independent Ireland in Comparative Perspective', *Irish Economic and Social History* 44, no. 1 (2017): 19–45; and Cormac Ó Gráda, *A Rocky Road: The Irish Economy since the 1920s* (Manchester: Manchester University Press, 1997).

6. Barry Eichengreen, 'Institutions and Economic Growth: Europe after World War II', in Nicholas Crafts and Gianni Toniolo (eds.), *Economic Growth in Europe since 1945* (Cambridge: Cambridge University Press, 1996), pp. 38–72.

7. O'Rourke, 'Independent Ireland in Comparative Perspective'.

8. John FitzGerald and Seán Kenny, 'Managing a Century of Debt', *Journal of the Statistical and Social Inquiry Society of Ireland*, 48 (2018–19): 1–40.

9. *Ibid.* p. 21.

10. In 1943 Labour won 15.7 per cent and in 1969 it won 17 per cent.

11. The major right parties in Ireland between 2007 and 2024 were Fianna Fáil, Fine Gael, Progressive Democrats and Aontú. Smaller right parties included: Direct Democracy Ireland, Renua, Wexford Independent Alliance, Irish Freedom Party, the National Party, Independent Ireland, the Irish People, and Ireland First. The major left parties were Labour, Sinn Féin, the Green Party, the Social Democrats, People Before Profit and the Socialist Party/Anti-Austerity Alliance. Smaller left parties included: the Workers' Party, Workers and Unemployed Action Group, United Left, Éirígí, Independents 4 Change, RISE, and the South Kerry Independent Alliance. Parties that failed to achieve 0.1 per cent of the vote in any election between 2007 and 2024 are counted but not listed here.

12. The discussion of the economic crisis and the austerity that followed draws in particular on Karl Whelan, 'Ireland's Economic Crisis: The Good, the Bad and the Ugly', *Journal of Macroeconomics* 39(Part B) (2014): 424–40.

13. *Ibid.*, p. 434.

14. Central Statistics Office, Expenditure on Gross and Net National Income at Current Market Prices, Annual National Accounts, https://data.cso.ie/table/NA007 (last accessed 28 June 2024).

15. John FitzGerald and Ide Kearney, 'Irish Government Debt and Implied Debt Dynamics: 2011–2015', *Quarterly Economic Commentary* 3 (Autumn 2011): 5.

16. *Ibid.*, p. 14.

17. Central Statistics Office, ILO Participation, Employment and Unemployment Characteristics, Labour Force Survey Quarterly Series, https://data.cso.ie/table/QLF18 (last accessed 28 June 2024).

18. Rory Hearne, 'Irish Austerity/Bailout/Recovery: Myths, Lies and Neoliberalism', National University of Ireland Maynooth, www.maynooth

university.ie/sites/default/files/assets/document/Hearne,%20Dr.%20 Rory%20Austerity_0.pdf (last accessed 28 June 2024).

19. Richard Layte and David Landy, 'The Fighting Irish? Explaining the Temporal Pattern of Social Protest during Ireland's Fiscal Crisis 2008–2014', *Sociology* 52, no. 6 (2018): 1270–89.

20. Irial Glynn, Tomás Kelly and Piaras Mac Einrí, 'The Re-Emergence of Emigration from Ireland: New Trends in An Old Story', Migration Policy Institute, 2015, www.migrationpolicy.org/sites/default/files/publications/ TCM-Emigration-Ireland-FINAL.pdf (last accessed 28 June 2024).

21. Central Statistics Office, Population Estimates (Persons in April), Annual Population Estimates, https://data.cso.ie/table/PEA01 (last accessed 28 June 2024).

22. Central Statistics Office, Estimated Migration (Persons in April), Annual Population Estimates, https://data.cso.ie/table/PEA03 (last accessed 28 June 2024).

23. Central Statistics Office, ILO Participation and Unemployment Rates, Labour Force Survey Quarterly Series, https://data.cso.ie/table/QLF02 (last accessed 28 June 2024).

24. Eurostat, Actual Individual Consumption, https://ec.europa.eu/eurostat/ databrowser/view/PRC_PPP_IND__custom_10763652/ (last accessed 26 February 2024).

25. See note 11.

26. Both Joan Collins and Clare Daly were previously leading members of the Socialist Party, while Séamus Healy had been a leading member of the League for a Workers' Republic.

27. Central Statistics Office, Residential Dwelling Property Transactions, https://data.cso.ie/table/HPA02 (last accessed 28 June 2024).

28. Residential Tenancies Board, Rent Index Q3, www.rtb.ie/images/ uploads/forms/RTB_Rent_Index_Q3_2023_Report.pdf (last accessed 28 June 2024).

29. Central Statistics Office, Average Earnings, Hours Worked, Employment and Labour Costs, Earnings Hours and Employment Costs Quarterly Survey, https://data.cso.ie/table/EHQ03 (last accessed 28 June 2024).

30. Sinn Féin, *Giving Workers and Families a Break: A Manifesto for Change*, Sinn Féin General Election Manifesto 2020, www.sinnfein.ie/files/2020/ Giving_Workers_and_Families_a_Break_-_A_Manifesto_for_Change. pdf (last accessed 28 June 2024).

31. Thirty-seven out of 42 candidates were elected.

32. William Hederman, 'The Shell to Sea Campaign and Its Legacy', *Rupture*, 27 March 2023, https://rupture.ie/articles/the-shell-to-sea-campaign-and-its-legacy (last accessed 28 June 2024).

PART I
Campaigns

2

Anti-Austerity Struggles 2008–13

David Landy

Perhaps nothing could have been done about it. Perhaps Ireland's fate was written on the night of 29 September 2008 when the government agreed to a full bailout of the banks without even knowing the scale of their losses. This decision inevitably led to Ireland becoming bankrupt a few years later and the government turning to the Troika of the European Central Bank (ECB), International Monetary Fund (IMF) and European Union (EU) to bail out the economy in November 2010. Equally inevitably, the Troika imposed strict conditionality on their loan, a harsh savings programme which directed the Irish government down the route of imposing austerity.

This chapter examines the development of opposition to this austerity from 2008 to 2013. It aims to provide some sort of order to the avalanche of events and campaigns of this time. I draw upon Niamh Hourigan's division of these years into three periods – the early unfocused, single-issue protests, the years of 'muted protest' from 2009 to 2011, led, if that is the word, by the Labour Party and trade unions.[1] Finally, from 2012 onwards, the years of popular opposition that began with the campaign against household charges, and which was signalled by the Occupy movement in late 2011.

In these years of catastrophe and powerlessness – from 2008 until 2013 when Ireland exited the bailout programme – the story of the Irish left can be framed as trying and failing to find ways to oppose the juggernaut of austerity. The process affected the moderate and radical left differently – weakening the former and strengthening the latter. This was because the moderate left – Labour Party and trade unions – were browbeaten into acceding to and indeed administering austerity, while the smaller radical left, consisting of left republicans, Trotskyists, anarchists and unaligned activists, continued fighting against it. At the time, however, it hardly seemed that the radical left had been strengthened – the fight had the characteristic of haphazard hyperactivity and involved the throwing up of a multiplicity of short-lived organisational forms whose collapse only further demoralised already exhausted activists.

Lacking the capacity, unity and public trust to effectively oppose austerity, these groups experienced this period as a chaotic time where they tried to develop these three elements and also to find the spark that would light the tinder of public grievances, a spark that seemed frustratingly out of reach.

MUTING THE PROTESTS – 'LABOUR'S WAY OR FRANKFURT'S WAY'

When the financial crash hit, those seeking alleviation from austerity and unemployment looked to the established left – trade unions, the Labour Party and, to a smaller extent, non-governmental organisations (NGOs). The NGOs, however, were largely dependent on government funding, and the government were adept at using this dependency as a disciplining mechanism. The closing down of Combat Poverty and the anti-racism body the National Consultative Committee on Racism and Interculturalism (NCCRI) in 2008 had a chilling effect on the sector. Some NGOs flirted with anti-government action – a couple of well-funded carnivalesque marches were organised by community development NGOs in December 2010 and 2011, called Spectacles of Defiance and Hope. But these small events were intentionally connected to no political forces – banners and leaflets were forbidden at them – and led nowhere. Indeed, community funding was almost halved during the recession.[2] There were a few other small initiatives such as the Anglo: Not Our Debt campaign of 2012, organised by development aid NGOs, which pushed for the government to renege on the bank guarantee. However, the real spectacle that NGOs put on in this period was one of quiescence and acquiescence, and overall their effect was, perhaps thankfully, negligible.

Niamh Hourigan notes that the first year of the crisis saw a number of single-issue demonstrations, such as the large pensioner and student protests that took place on the same day in October 2008. However, she argues that these protests dried up once the public realised the magnitude of the banking crisis, and they were replaced by years of 'muted protest'.[3] Certainly, there was a sense of powerlessness at the scale and suddenness of the economic crash, a degree of acceptance of the official narrative that during the Celtic Tiger 'we all partied' and thus we all had to suffer for it.[4] The role of emigration in providing a literal escape valve also played a part in muting opposition. From 2009 to the end of 2013, Ireland lost 106,000 people to emigration, increasing the sense of hopelessness and decreasing the likelihood of protest. However, the muting of opposition was also due to the influence of the Labour Party and trade unions, which contained protest and channelled anti-government anger down institutional routes from 2009 to 2011.

When the crisis hit, the Labour Party offered strident rhetorical denunciations of austerity and promises to 'burn the bondholders' – that is, to refuse to pay the debts of the banks to international bondholders – should they get into power. They made a straightforward offer to the electorate in early 2011 to choose a Labour government as an alternative to rule by the Troika, with the slogan, 'It's Labour's Way or Frankfurt's way' – Frankfurt being the home of the ECB. Voters took them up on this, giving the party their best ever election result and propelling them into government as junior partner with Fine Gael.

Once in government, the Labour Party quickly found itself administering austerity and carefully following Frankfurt's way, neither burning bondholders nor even – in the parlance of the time – 'giving them a haircut'. Despite this, the new government retained a huge amount of goodwill. The crisis was clearly not their fault, and because of the severity of the economic crisis and the holes in government finance, the harsh austerity measures they took were seen as both forced by the Troika and, while painful, necessary. This honeymoon period lasted for much of 2011, as evinced by the election of the Labour Party stalwart Michael D. Higgins as president of Ireland in October 2011 and the party's by-election success in Dublin West the same day. Labour Party ministers were not shy about their role, and the role of electoralism more generally, in muting popular protest. Witness prominent Labour Party representative, Ruairi Quinn, speaking of the 2011 elections: 'Unlike Greece, Spain and Portugal where there were riots in the streets and all sorts of disruptions, the people held their breaths and waited for the ballot box and dropped the grenade silently into the ballot box.'[5]

The role of the union movement in muting protest was equally important. Trade unions used popular discontent as a bargaining chip to bolster up their weak position in negotiations over wage reductions. There was a one-day strike of public servants in November 2009 over threatened pay cuts and 250,000 workers took part in the first such strike for over 20 years. However, with the union leadership accepting the inevitability of such cuts, there was no follow-up to this once-off strike. Instead of workplace mobilisations, the unions organised large anti-austerity marches in February 2009 and November 2010 of about 100,000 each. However, for many attendees, the demonstrations were dispiriting and pointless outings to let off steam rather than to build anti-austerity campaigns. After Labour was elected, the Irish Congress of Trade Unions (ICTU), much of whose leadership was aligned with the Labour Party, waited till February 2013 to call another march. This was a relatively poorly attended affair – about 30,000 in Dublin and 20,000 more around the country – that proved less a demonstration of strength than an exhibition of how alienated the union leaders were from those they purported to lead. At the Dublin event, ICTU speakers vacated the stage in favour of musicians before many of the marchers had arrived at the destination, so as not to be heckled. Stewards were instructed to section off leftwing campaigners from the rest of the march. Barely able to contain the left, even at their own events, this was to be the last ICTU demonstration of the crisis.

By then, Ireland had earned a well-deserved reputation for passivity in the face of austerity. One of the chants of the Greek protestors of 2010 was, 'we are not Ireland. We will resist' – a fact referenced time and again on the left in Ireland.[6] By 2012, government ministers were openly sneering that Ireland was indeed not like Greece,[7] and academics could earnestly wonder why the Irish weren't rebelling.[8] This was a straightforward consequence of the established organs of the left failing to oppose, or worse, administering austerity programmes. The torch, perhaps inevitably, would be passed to the far left.

EARLY FAR-LEFT INITIATIVES – THE 1% AND THE 99%

The radical left wasn't inactive during this early period, the recession having led to an admixture of pessimism and revolutionary optimism. On one hand, many believed that once austerity had been structured into the economy there would be few options for meaningful resistance, and thus there was the sense of a door closing on the opportunities to effect change. On the other, there was optimism at the uptick in actual opposition. As mentioned in Chapter 1, social protest was at a low ebb in the years before the recession. All of a sudden there was a rush of significant demonstrations, mobilisations and workplace activism. Pensioners, farmers, civil servants and taxi drivers all launched huge protests in 2009. Apart from strikes, militant workplace occupations in Waterford Crystal, Visteon in Derry and Thomas Cook in Dublin led to a feeling that the fightback against austerity was mobilising new constituencies. This mix of despair and optimism led to a perhaps frenetic effort to organise and campaign.

The radical left groups faced the problem of extremely limited resources, organisation and reach – their demonstrations never numbered more than a couple of thousand people, their organisations remained tiny and their statements rarely received any media uptake. This period can then be seen as a series of attempts to find a form to anti-austerity campaigning that would tap into the society-wide discontent that was being widely voiced but was not finding an organised political expression. For groups accustomed to being on the fringes of society and speaking mostly to – and against – others on the left, this would prove an insurmountable task.

Symptomatic of such efforts was the Right to Work campaign. By 2010, unemployment had jumped to 14 per cent, and, in response, with one eye on the upcoming elections, the Socialist Workers Party (SWP) established a Right to Work campaign in mid-2010 with the union Unite – one of the few unions not aligned to the Labour Party. While they had a national conference on 22 May, they had little strategies besides weekly marches on the Dáil. The first demonstration on 11 May had over a thousand attendees and a roster of speakers including prominent journalists, several trade unionists and community workers.[9] Inevitably thereafter though, the demonstrations declined, petering out to about 300 attendees in June. However, on the back of these marches, an anti-capitalist bloc was formed on these demos. The chief movers in this were the anarchist organisation the Workers Solidarity Movement (WSM) and the socialist republican party Éirígí.

These groups developed The 1% Network out of this bloc, an anti-capitalist network. About a year before Occupy burst onto the scene, the radical left in Ireland had identified the division as being between the 99 per cent and 1 per cent. However, rather than identifying with the 99 per cent as a force for change, which Occupy would do, the focus was on the 1 per cent as a target for anger. This was perhaps symptomatic of their oppositional consciousness, as well as their experience of being marginal and sidelined. The 1% Network tried to break out of the usual round of marches to the Dáil, and organised a few walking tours and some street theatre in the autumn of 2010 and spring of 2011 in order to try and build interest in anti-capitalism.[10] However, these events garnered little traction.

The contained nature of protest in Ireland of the time stood in sharp contrast with elsewhere in Europe. There was occasional pushing and shoving between Gardaí and protestors, but nothing like the riots in other countries. For instance, at the Right to Work protest on 11 May 2010, a few protestors dashed past the police into the grounds of the Dáil, something seen as so outrageous to make news headlines.[11] A few days later, an Éirígí protest at Anglo Irish Bank was attacked by police (see Chapter 10 on republicanism), in September of that year a cement lorry was used to block the gates of the Dáil. But these were just sporadic confrontations with the police. The only serious violence came when a large student protest on 3 November 2010 occupied the foyer of the Department of Finance, and here the violence came from Gardaí, rather than protestors.[12]

34

The establishment of Occupy camps in Dublin, Belfast, Cork, Galway and Waterford in October 2011 was the first intimation that this era of social pacification was coming to an end. It's difficult to remember the enthusiasm with which the Occupy movement was greeted in Ireland because of the ill-tempered farce into which it degenerated. Drawing from Occupy Wall St in the US, which was in turn inspired by previous occupations in Egypt in 2010 and the movement of the squares in Spain and Greece in summer 2011, protestors occupied the plaza in front of the Central Bank in Dame Street, Dublin on 8 October 2011. They sought to create a public square where people could both demonstrate their opposition to the failed governing system and to discuss and articulate new alternatives to it. With its central slogan, 'We are the 99%' (versus the 1 per cent), Occupy's aim was to create a mass participatory movement through direct democratic means. In this spirit, discussions and workshops quickly sprang up on Dame Street, a small library was established, and donations collected to enable people to keep camping in the space. Despite the initial goodwill, Occupy Dame Street never broke out of the left/alternative bubble and was hamstrung by a spirit of anti-politics and a near absolute mistrust of all political forms, which polluted discourse at the time. As Richard McAlaevey noted,

> Rather than having absolute democracy as the horizon, what seemed to take hold was a fear of the Socialist Workers Party (or similar) coming along and turning it into Marxism On Dame Street. And so there was a ban on political parties and party political literature, which rubbed quite a lot of people up the wrong way.[13]

One of the turning points for Occupy Dame Street was a fractious meeting on November 8 during which the camp refused a request to co-organise an anti-austerity march with the Dublin Council of Trade Unions later that month, partly out of frustration with SWP intervention but also because of anti-union sentiment.[14] While this hostility towards unions and the established left may have been particularly acute in Dublin – the camp in Cork was a comparatively more convivial affair – the central problem was one experienced by the Occupy movement around the world. The movement frequently became transfixed on the process of maintaining and running the Occupy camp rather than fostering a popular movement of opposition and solidarity. A division developed with full-time campers – always more drawn from the alternative fringe – becoming progressively alienated from part-time participants and indeed the world outside the camp. While the camps in Ireland persisted throughout the winter, they had lost their relevance, and many on the left heaved a guilty sigh of relief when the police finally evicted the Occupy Dame Street camp in March 2012. The camp in Cork voluntarily left a few days later, and though the Galway camp lasted till May, Occupy had already been consigned to the ranks of yet another failed experiment.

CAHWT IN A TRAP – 'DON'T REGISTER – DON'T PAY'

Although Occupy created a flurry of interest, it was not as significant as the Campaign Against the Household and Water Taxes (CAHWT), established in reaction to the long-awaited household charges announced in the December 2011 budget.[15] The household charge was initially a relatively modest flat rate of €100 a year in order to encourage people to register – the plan was to follow this up with a more severe property tax the following year. Mobilising against these charges was the primary focus of the left in 2012. And although the campaign was comprehensively defeated, it ushered in unprecedented electoral success for the far left and a new period of popular mobilisation from 2014 onwards.

CAHWT had already been launched in summer 2011 as a broad umbrella grouping of the left. The campaign began in earnest a week after the budget announcement with a press conference, where nine leftwing TDs urged a boycott of the charges. Virtually every leftwing group was a member and this was by far the largest leftwing campaign of the period, which almost, but not quite, took the form of mass mobilisation.

The only major left party to not participate fully was Sinn Féin. While some Sinn Féin TDs announced they weren't paying the household charges, others said they were. The party didn't advocate a boycott, but said they supported people who weren't paying.[16]

Individual Sinn Féin members were active in CAHWT, though the party wasn't a member. This form of partial (non-)commitment proved to be the defining feature of Sinn Féin's approach to most political struggles of the time.

The campaign started strongly, partly because it drew upon existing branch networks of the political parties involved. At times, the local CAHWT organisation was little more than the constituency group of whichever party was most dominant in the area and was used to recruit for that party. While this would fuel popular distrust of how Trotskyist parties used the campaign, it provided an instant footfall for CAHWT. The campaign also benefited from having a clear strategy about how to counter the charges – one inherited from the successful fight against the water charges in Dublin in the 1990s – a strategy of mass non-payment, organised through door knocking, public meetings and local campaign groups. While the weakness of this strategy would emerge, initially it worked well and there were campaign groups – at least on paper – throughout the 26 counties. By 31 March 2012, the deadline for registration, only about half of households had registered to pay. Campaigners were jubilant and talked of a campaign with a million non-payers. Besides organising locally for non-payment, the campaign had also mobilised large numbers at a march to the Fine Gael Ard Fheis (national conference) in Dublin on 31 March, and to a raucous demonstration at the Labour Party's conference in Galway two weeks later, where Gardaí pepper sprayed the demonstrators.[17] By April, some unions – such as Unite and the Civil and Public Services Union (CPSU) – had officially joined the campaign and were calling for non-payment.[18]

However, while people were happy to passively not pay the charges, especially when the fines for doing so were small, internal tensions between Trotskyist parties and others meant the campaign was too weak to respond successfully to government countermeasures in 2013. In addition, though some unions had joined, there was growing animosity between the leadership of the Labour-aligned union movement and CAHWT. These divisions and weaknesses meant that when the government passed legislation in December 2012 that would allow them to deduct it directly from people's wages, the campaign did not have the strength to respond properly. The campaign had been expecting non-payers would be taken to court, which would have provided an arena of struggle. But instead of giving them their days in court, the government simply deducted the money at source. In response, CAHWT began a strategy to occupy council chambers in February 2013, and this was done in Dublin, Galway, Cork, Kilkenny and Athlone, among other places. There were also small-scale pickets outside offices of revenue commissioners and one temporary occupation in Dublin in May 2013. But these were small-scale events and the campaign was unable to institute a wider campaign of civil disobedience.

In the face of deduction at source, the boycott tactic was rendered useless and with a compliance rate at 90 per cent by June 2013, the campaign was effectively defeated. Unsurprisingly, CAHWT – always an uneasy alliance – became riven with internal fighting. In their statement of 26 June 2013, announcing their departure from the campaign, WSM declared that the campaign's tactics – non-payment and civil disobedience – were correct, but they had failed because it didn't have mass participation. They blamed this on the campaign being diverted into electoralism by the Socialist Party (SP).[19] The SP did indeed want to turn CAHWT into an electoral vehicle and, in a bitterly contested decision at the CAHWT national conference of April 2013, they managed to get the organisation to agree to endorse candidates for the oncoming local elections and to make defeating the Labour Party an aspect of the campaign. After CAHWT's collapse, the SP in turn attacked others in the campaign for failing to follow their electoralist policy, which they argued would have widened the campaign.[20]

THE SEARCH FOR A BROAD LEFT PARTY

This sorry story illustrates a central feature of the Irish left in this period – its organisational disunity. It's perhaps surprising that no lasting political organisations were born in this time of political turmoil beyond fringe, temporary initiatives. That said, there was one noteworthy effort to form a grouping that had the possibility to become a broad left party – the United Left Alliance (ULA), which lasted slightly over two years.

This began as a simple electoral alliance in November 2010 between the SP, SWP and the smaller Tipperary-based Workers and Unemployed Action Group (WUAG), in time for the February 2011 general election. Its first conference, a packed-out affair in Liberty Hall[21] on 27 June 2011, reached beyond the two Trotskyist groups that were its main composition and showed the thirst for a broad left alliance. With structures that allowed for the representation and participation of non-aligned leftists, there were hopes it would develop beyond a simple electoral alliance into having an independent identity, and several hundred non-aligned members had joined by 2012.

However, these hopes were dashed, mainly because both the SWP and SP wished to promote their own separate parties within the broad alliance, rather than let it develop its own political identity. The lack of commitment to developing the ULA by the two main constituent groups proved fatal. In January 2012, the SP publicly announced their party's scepticism about the capacity of the ULA to transform into a party.[22] The SWP was more supportive of developing the ULA, although one commentator argued that the only difference was 'the SWP viewed the alliance as a "popular front" to recruit from while the SP viewed it as solely an electoral alliance, neither wanting the ULA as such to develop into a party'.[23]

By then, non-aligned members of the ULA had found themselves sidelined when it came to decision making, with the grouping carved up between the SWP and SP, both of whom possessed a veto in decision making. The carve-up grew increasingly dysfunctional as internal fights within the SP – specifically the departure of one of its TDs, Clare Daly – spilled out into the ULA. By October 2012 the WUAG left the ULA, to be followed in early 2013 by the SP. With the hope for a left alliance over, the SP would seek to use the name Anti-Austerity Alliance as a wider front to draw in members and voters, and the SWP would do the same with People Before Profit, albeit with greater success.

In the fallout from the collapse of the ULA and of CAHWT, a number of independent or, rather, homeless leftwingers began an initiative in February 2013 called the Left Forum. The aim was to examine the possibility of a left organisation that would not become another tiny vanguardist party. While the initiative garnered a lot of goodwill, the central problem remained – what would such an organisation do if it were not to compete for votes? In the end it organised and advertised a few discussion groups and talks, and a debate in November 2013 about whether a new political party was needed. Following this, a number of its leading lights, including three of the eight-person coordinating committee, departed to try to revitalise the once powerful but now near-defunct Worker's Party, which had its heyday in the 1980s. This surprising move can be seen as yet another attempt to create a broad left grouping that would finally burst out of the confines of small sectarian parties. As Gavin Mendel-Gleeson, one of the initiators of the move to the Workers' Party optimistically wrote of it, 'The DNA required to be a mass party is still there. It's merely a question of revitalisation rather than having to craft it from scratch.'[24] While the gamble may have been worth taking, the Worker's Party, despite modest growth, failed to come anywhere near being the mass party its new members yearned for.

So, while it's tempting to speculate on what might have happened had a unitary left party arisen in this time, the left remained as fragmented and sectarian as before, with many sections of it – after five years fighting austerity with no apparent results – more demoralised than ever.

CONCLUSION

> There are activists who are demoralised, supporters likewise, a government that has seen it can impose its will and will be making every effort to ensure the implementation of water meters and charges is such that it isn't open to messing about and so on and so forth. And let's not forget that the broader context is one of ULA collapse, open sniping on the further left.[25]

It is difficult to overstate the feeling of exhaustion and disillusion in late 2013. The bulk of the union movement, still aligned, however unhappily, with the austerity-implementing Labour Party, had been browbeaten into accepting worsening pay and conditions for public sector workers with the Haddington Road agreement (see Chapter 6 on unions). The radical left had been comprehensively defeated on the one anti-austerity struggle they'd seriously fought – household taxes. More than that, they'd been discredited, having been easily outmanoeuvred by the government, and shown themselves to be strategically inept and hopelessly divided. There was mistrust in working-class communities at how the Trotskyist parties had abandoned the property tax campaign, mistrust which shaded into anger among those who had been sanctioned for not paying the tax.

All attempts to form structures to combat austerity had run into either the swamp of left sectarianism or the sands of public indifference. The former had doomed the ULA, while the latter had done for the ephemeral organisations and initiatives from the non-aligned and anarchist left. The public mood was judged to be sullen but compliant – judged not simply by the lack of participation in attempts to mobilise them but in practical measures, for instance, through paying the property tax. Another example of this sullen compliance was the popular vote in favour of the EU fiscal treaty in a June 2012 referendum, even though this treaty restricted the possibility of future government spending. Andy Storey of the Campaign Against the Austerity Treaty (CAAT) may have been correct in saying that the public were blackmailed into voting yes, since the clearly stated threat was that Ireland would lose access to European loans if it voted no.[26] But the point remained, the blackmail was successful.

Different groups had different responses to their failure. Trotskyist parties tended to blame others on the left – mainly unions and the Labour Party – and saw no reason to change their strategies.[27] This was strategically sound; their electoralist approach was beginning to bear fruit, as was their targeting of the Labour Party. Moreover, they remained confident in their tactics, something which enabled them to keep on keeping on. However, among the anarchist left, who had poured their hearts into a dozen vehicles and organisational forms, all of which died from lack of resources or outside interest, the feeling of despair was strongest. They began to drop out of politics or look for alternative political forms. As an article in the *Irish Anarchist Review* stated: 'the period of struggle from 2008-2014 suggests that there is less strength in building struggles around broad "bread & butter" issues than we imagined and a suggestion that diversity proved more useful in sustaining progressive struggle.'[28]

As to what this diversity might entail, for some the occupation of a large derelict site by several dozen squatters in August 2013, and the creation of a Squat City in Grangegorman near Dublin city centre seemed a harbinger of the future. Squat City, which functioned as a social centre, was both a political move and at the same time a retreat from attempts to influence the outside world, in favour of building up a 'beloved community'.

In retrospect, it's easy to say they were wrong. Squat City was evicted in June 2015, and while the practical skills gained in the effort were used by the nascent housing movement and in the spread of squatting throughout Dublin – squatting was a way out of politics, rather than towards the politics of the future. Instead, Ireland was on the cusp of the largest 'bread and butter issues' movement it had ever seen and in this we can see the anti-austerity campaigning of 2008–13 not as the failure it seemed at the time but a necessary precursor.

A proper balance sheet would recognise how the Labour Party and the aligned section of the union movement were rendered powerless to influence or sidetrack the anti-austerity movement. This was partly due to Labour's record in administering austerity and the effect of gaffes such as the 2013 removal of medical cards from disabled children. But it was also the effect of constant attacks on the party from the left, and their attacks in turn on the anti-austerity movement. Inverting their 'It's Labour's Way or Frankfurt's Way' election slogan and referring to Garda tactics at their 2012 conference, the leftwing taunt became, 'It's Labour's Way or Pepper Spray.' Alienation from the electorate would follow. Labour was still polling in the mid-teens in 2012, a respectable figure considering they received 19 per cent in the 2011 general election. They slumped further in 2013, but even still were ill-prepared to receive 7 per cent of the vote and a loss of most of their seats in the 2014 local elections.

The defanging of the Labour Party stood in contrast to the success of the radical left in these elections. While anarchists may have decried how CAHWT was used to promote radical left candidates throughout the country, there is no denying it was a successful strategy. The 2014 elections were a victory for leftwing independents and Trotskyist parties alike. One of the reasons was CAHWT's network of dozens of local groups up and down the country, mobilising an activist base that moved beyond Dublin and demonstrating the increased capacity of the far left. Aiding this capacity was slowly changing relations with trade unions. Though the mutual hostility with the Labour-aligned leadership of ICTU and SIPTU was unabated, there was the seed of cooperation with other trade unions, themselves seeking to move away from the years of muted protest. An indication of this future lay in the demonstration jointly organised by CAHWT and the Dublin Council of Trade Unions in November 2012 that bought 12,000 out on the street to protest austerity. The revolutionary optimism of 2009 may have been misplaced, but so was the paralleled pessimism of 2013.

NOTES

1. Niamh Hourigan, 'Austerity, Resistance and Social Protest in Ireland: Movement Outcomes', in Emma Heffernan, Niamh Moore-Cherry and John McHale (eds.), *Debating Austerity: Crisis, Experience and Recovery* (Dublin: Royal Irish Academy, 2017), pp. 115–28.
2. Rory Hearne, 'The Irish Water War, Austerity and the "Risen People"', Maynooth University, 2015, p. 19, www.maynoothuniversity.ie/sites/default/files/assets/document/TheIrishWaterwar_0.pdf (all URLs last accessed August 2024).
3. Hourigan 'Austerity', pp. 117–18.
4. At the same time, large single-issue protests continued during the early years of recession, for example, the student demonstration in November 2010 (circa 30,000 protestors) or the Waterford hospital protest in November 2012 (circa 12,000 protestors).
5. '"Ireland Was a Shipwreck ... We Had to Do Things We Did Not Want to Do" – Labour's Pat Rabbitte', *Irish Independent*, 25 May 2014.
6. Some examples: Vincent Browne, 'Irish Inertia No Match for Greek Resistance', *Magill*, 9 May 2010, https://magill.ie/politics/irish-inertia-no-match-greek-resistance; *Look Left*, 'This Is Greece, Not Ireland', 10 April 2012, www.lookleft.ie/2012/04/this-is-greece-not-ireland/.
7. Marie O'Halloran, 'Feta Cheese Remarks Reasonable, Says Noonan', *Irish Times*, May 24, 2012.
8. Barry Cannon and Mary P. Murphy, 'Where Are the Pots and Pans? Collective Responses in Ireland to Neoliberalization in a Time of Crisis:

Learning from Latin America', *Irish Political Studies* 30, no. 1 (2014): 1–19, https://doi.org/10.1080/07907184.2014.942292; Takis S. Pappas and Eoin O'Malley, 'Civil Compliance and "Political Luddism": Explaining Variance in Social Unrest during Crisis in Ireland and Greece', *American Behavioral Scientist* 58, no. 12 (2014): 1592–613, https://doi.org/10.1177/0002764214534663.

9. Joseph Galvin, 'Minor Skirmish Mars Anti-government Protest', *Magill*, 11 May 2010, https://magill.ie/politics/minor-skirmish-mars-anti-government-protest.

10. WSM, 'What Was the 1% Network?' 15 June 2015, www.wsm.ie/c/what-was-1-network.

11. RTE, 'Protest at Dáil over Bank Bailout', 12 May 2010. www.rte.ie/news/2010/0511/130879-dail/.

12. Stacy Wrenn, 'Former Student Activists Look Back on Garda Brutality and USI Neglect in Wake of 2010 March', *Trinity News*, 26 December 2016, https://tinyurl.com/2798pupv.

13. Richard McAlaevey, 'Notes on Occupy Dame Street', *Cunning Hired Knaves Blog*, 5 March 2013, https://hiredknaves.wordpress.com/2013/03/05/notes-on-occupy-dame-street/.

14. Helena Sheehan, 'Occupying Dublin: Considerations at the Crossroads', Dublin City University, 2012, https://doras.dcu.ie/16847/1/Occupying_Dublin_HS_1-11.pdf.

15. The final official name of this charge is the 'Local Property Tax'.

16. 'Pearse Doherty Won't Pay Household Charge – But Says Don't Follow His Lead', *The Journal*, 16 December 2011, https://tinyurl.com/zvewrwk2.

17. It's telling that, four years into the crisis, this was the first time pepper spray was used at a demonstration.

18. Anne Marie Walsh, 'Unions Encourage Civil Disobedience against Property Tax', *Irish Independent*, 6 April 2013.

19. WSM, 'Statement from Workers Solidarity Movement: Why We Are Leaving Campaign Against Home and Water Taxes', 26 June 2013, https://tinyurl.com/2xh7mf95.

20. Ruth Coppinger, 'Property and Water Taxes: What's Needed Now to Fight Austerity?' Socialist Party website, 6 December 2013, https://tinyurl.com/5y9xjee8.

21. Liberty Hall is the home of Irish trade unionism, and the headquarters of the largest Irish union, Services, Industrial, Professional and Technical Union (SIPTU). Its auditorium seats over 400.

22. Socialist Party, 'What Next for the United Left Alliance?' Socialist Party website, 17 January 2012. www.socialistparty.ie/2012/01/what-next-for-the-united-left-alliance/.

23. Henry Silke, 'The Socialist Party Leaves the United Left Alliance', Tomás Ó Flatharta blog, 29 January 2013 https://tinyurl.com/bddk9ccv.

24. Gavin Mendel-Gleeson, 'Why the Workers' Party', Spirit of Contradiction blog, 21 January 2015, https://spiritofcontradiction.eu/rowan-duffy/2015/01/21/why-the-workers-party.
25. WorldbyStorm, '[Comment]', Cedar Lounge Revolution blog, 27 June 2013, https://tinyurl.com/bds34k7.
26. Andy Storey, 'An Explicit Campaign of Blackmail Waged against Potential "No" Voters', CAAT press release, 1 June 2012, https://tinyurl.com/rksthatj.
27. For instance: Socialist Party, 'Take the Fight against Austerity on to the Political Field', 16 July 2013, https://tinyurl.com/5xw7598p.
28. Andrew Flood, 'Turnips Hammers and Squares', *Irish Anarchist Review* 10 (Summer 2014): 5.

3

Water Charges

Dave Gibney

INTRODUCTION

The Irish government of Fianna Fáil and the Green Party agreed in 2010 to implement domestic water charges. Despite what many believe, it was not a condition of support from the Troika or the EU but was entirely an Irish government decision. Fine Gael and Labour were elected in 2011 on the back of opposition to austerity. Despite this, the two parties wholeheartedly supported the proposition of a regressive regime of domestic water charges which would inevitably lead to privatisation, and this was on top of hundreds of other austerity measures. The already hard-pressed Irish public weren't about to take this lying down – and so began one of the world's largest and most energetic protest movements.

There are three general ways to pay for domestic water usage: through domestic water charges, a rates-based system like the north of Ireland, and through general taxation. The Republic of Ireland has a long history of paying for our domestic water use through general taxation, which is progressive and fair because those with the most wealth, who generally use the most, pay the most. There have been several battles in the past to prevent the imposition of domestic water charges, most notably in the 1970s and 1990s. It's fair to say that the battle to prevent domestic water charges, past and present, has been a battle to prevent the privatisation of our water.

Water has become one of the most profitable non-financial assets in the world, and many large multinational water and financial companies would love the opportunity to enter the Irish 'market' and exploit it. This was illustrated on the Credit Suisse website, which boastfully stated: 'Water is Scarce, But the Profits Aren't.'

With rapid population growth and a worrying growth in water scarcity – where the UN now predicts that five billion people, or around two-thirds of the world's population, will face at least one month of water shortages by 2050 – capitalists are preparing to exploit the very essence of life. In 2011, Citigroup chief economist Willem Buiter said: 'Water as an asset class will, in my view, become eventually the single most important physical-commodity-based asset class, dwarfing oil, copper, agriculture commodities, and precious metals.' Ten years later, commenting on his own prediction, he chillingly added, 'the future is now'.[1]

Paying for water through progressive general taxation means there's no water poverty (when a household spends more than 3 per cent of income on water) in Ireland. None. That's compared to almost all other developed countries, including those with comparable climates like England, which has a water poverty level of 17.4 per cent, and Wales with 27.2 per cent. It also means no water shut-offs for families who cannot afford their bills, like those we regularly see in the United States and in other countries in the EU, including Italy and France.

RIGHT2WATER

From the outset it's important to note the differences between the anti-water charges movement and the Right2Water campaign. The anti-water charges movement began in earnest around February 2014 in Togher, Co. Cork. The Ballyphehan/South Parish Says No group decided to take a stand and block the installation of water meters in the Ashbrook estate. One woman in a middle-class housing estate in Dublin saw this and posted a message on her Facebook page asking for assistance in blocking the installation of water meters. Dozens of working-class people flocked to her aid. It then sent a ripple across the country, leading to the birth of one tactic of the anti-water charges movement.

Week after week, scandals arose in Irish Water and the government parties. From John Tierney announcing that Irish Water was splashing out €50 million on consultants, to Joan Burton's: 'All of the protesters that I have seen before seem to have extremely expensive phones, tablets, video cameras.'[2] Luckily, the job of agitating working-class communities was being done by those attempting to implement water charges. But was there a way to harness the emerging anger? Richard Boyd Barrett TD thought so.

On 2 June 2014, he called a meeting in the Dáil for political representatives and trade unions who had been prominent in the anti-austerity movement. Present was Boyd Barrett himself, Ruth Coppinger TD, Thomas Pringle TD, Joan Collins TD, Councillor Daithí Doolan for Sinn Féin and Independent Councillor Brendan Young. There were only two trade unions present, Unite the Union, with Brendan Ogle, Jimmy Kelly and Richie Brown, and Mandate Trade Union, represented by myself. Mandate and Unite largely represent low-paid workers. Mandate predominantly represents retail workers and Unite is a general workers' union.

At the meeting there was an extensive and often tense debate about the potential for a campaign. I argued against any campaign that was framed in a negative way. I felt many people were not only fed up with negativity but that the big hammer the media and establishment use against the left is that we are always against everything and never have solutions. So we developed Right2Water as a brand. A positive call. We wanted to fund our water services through general taxation, which is progressive and fair.

We also tried to make the campaign as broad as possible by establishing two key demands required to participate in the Right-2Water movement:

1. You must believe that water is a human right.
2. You must want to abolish water charges.

After the meeting it was agreed that Brendan Ogle and I would meet to formulate a plan around the campaign and bring back a presentation to the political group.

The first task was to identify the organisations who may be supportive of our campaign. So far, we only had two unions and a number of political parties. We needed to broaden the support. I collated the email addresses of all trade unions in the Republic of Ireland, along with many civil society organisations and charities. We sent an invite to almost 500 groups to the launch of the campaign in the Gresham Hotel in Dublin. We also invited the media. Only the *Irish Independent* turned up, but the turnout from civil society was encouraging. Addressing the meeting was Kathleen Lynch, a prominent University College Dublin professor with expertise on inequality.

In the audience, we had Amnesty International, who were very supportive of our initiative that day but never showed up again. The Civil and Public Services Union (CPSU) also turned up, and they then officially endorsed the campaign.

We then developed a website which contained a petition embedded in it. We knew we wouldn't receive much support from the mainstream media, so we wanted to be able to reach supporters without the need for social media advertising or newspaper columns. When we launched the petition, we received over 70,000 signatures and through that we had tens of thousands of email addresses to advertise upcoming demonstrations.

The first demonstration was announced for 11 October 2014. The trade unions paid for 500,000 flyers to be printed, with Moira Murphy, a talented graphic designer and a Mandate Trade Union organiser, preparing the graphics. Those flyers were distributed by all of the political parties and trade unions, and sent the message out in a way that we hadn't seen from any anti-austerity movement to date. Unite's researcher at the time, Michael Taft, prepared ten facts about water charges to kill off some of the economic arguments of those in favour of domestic charges. All of this was to provide activists and members of the public with ammunition to spread the word about the upcoming demonstration. These facts and posts were promoted on our social media pages, which had taken off like nothing we had seen before. The organic reach of Right2Water Ireland on Facebook alone went beyond 500,000 in the week leading up to the protest.

We expected big numbers, but generally in the 10,000–20,000 range. So, too, did the Gardaí. What happened that day was momentous. Upwards of 100,000 people came onto the streets. For scale, that's the equivalent of 1.5 million marching in London or 8 million marching in Washington.

The first Right2Water demonstration was an incredible success, but it wasn't perfect. There was abuse of stewards before the event had even begun. One 'activist' threw a punch at a steward wearing a trade union vest. Richard Boyd Barrett TD and I calmed things down a bit, but when Jimmy Kelly, regional secretary for Unite, got up to speak, there were boos from the crowd. He was the only trade union speaker other than Brendan Ogle, who was host on the day. It was very evident that many of those present didn't trust trade unions.

As a result, Brendan Ogle set up a meeting with some of the Says No groups who we were told were responsible for the anti-union sentiment but who were also leading the blockading of water meter installations in local communities. The meeting took place in the Edenmore House bar the following Tuesday. We had been told we would be meeting approximately 17 of the Says No group activists, but there were closer to 70 when we started the meeting. The room was filled with hostility. Many felt the trade union movement hadn't done enough to protect working-class communities from austerity. Brendan belted out his and Unite's credentials in fighting against austerity. He narrated a long history of his defences of workers' terms and conditions as a train driver and the pensions of Electricity Supply Board (ESB) workers. He also made it known that he grew up in a working-class community, just like theirs, and that, at times, he felt let down by the trade union movement. He pointed at me from the stage and explained my credentials too. It resonated. From that day on there was respect between the unions and the community groups.

Directly after that meeting in the Edenmore House bar, Brendan and I had to travel to Navan for a public meeting which had been organised by Peadar Tóibín TD and a number of local activists. Also involved was Seamus McDonagh from the Workers' Party. Seamus was also on the small organising group that had been established to plan the Right2Water campaign. This group consisted of approximately 15 individuals including me (Mandate Trade Union), Brendan Ogle (Unite), Des Fagan (CPSU), Cormac O'Dhalaigh (Communication Workers Union – CWU), Billy Wall (Operative Plasterers and Allied Trades Society of Ireland – OPATSI), Alex Klemm (Unite), Eugene McCartan (Communist Party of Ireland),

James O'Toole (People Before Profit), Rhona McCord (Clare Daly TD), Paddy Healy (WUAG), Deirdre Wadding (People Before Profit), Daithí Doolan (Sinn Féin), Richard Boyd Barrett TD, Bríd Smith TD, Joan Collins TD, Donal Higgins and Brendan Young, among others.

On the way to Navan, Brendan and I had a chat about the direction of the campaign, during which I proposed we use the Trademark Belfast organisation, who are the Irish Congress of Trade Union's anti-sectarian unit, to provide political economy training on the history of capitalism and where workers fit into the system. Over the coming months they provided hundreds of activists with education related to the financial crisis and why it was being used to speed up the privatisation agenda for almost all public utilities and state assets. This would be the start of the deep organising that took place ahead of the 2016 general election and probably the most important legacy of the campaign.

The next demonstration was organised for Saturday 1 November 2014. Right2Water had called for local demonstrations in every city, town and village in the country. There was great excitement and energy on the back of the first demo, but the sectarian nature of the Irish left was still a challenge, with some political parties refusing to work collectively with others. We had an idea. What if we used the leverage of this new brand of Right2Water and the energy behind it to encourage some of the political parties to work together? We told all parties and unions that we would only promote demonstrations that had been organised by more than two groups. If Mandate activists organised an event in Kerry, for example, they'd have to work with Sinn Féin or People Before Profit before we'd upload the event to the website. Before long, local representatives from each of the groups were sending me emails requesting that I upload their demonstration details on the website. Soon we had 46 events listed. It reached 106 on the day of the demo. There were only two locations where we couldn't get the parties to work together, but our conflict resolution skills kicked in. We managed to get activists from the Socialist Party and Sinn Féin, who refused to march together, to assemble in different locations and march to the same end point as a compromise.

The 1 November protest was even bigger than the first. We estimated almost 200,000 had turned out across the country. The government responded by attempting to take the wind out of our sails by implementing concessions. They capped the water bills at €260 – but this just raised more eyebrows because it meant the hundreds of millions being spent on water meters were wasted. It also made nonsense of the green argument that charges were being introduced to limit consumption. We were confident the changes to the water regime wouldn't have the impact the government expected. Minister Michael Noonan was confident too. He said the protesters were 'having their last rally around the water issue'.[3] How wrong he was.

We called the next demonstration for 10 December, which was International Human Rights Day, but it was also a Wednesday, making this a different type of challenge. It was an opportunity to hold a protest outside the Dáil, which would be open that day, unlike the previous two demonstrations, which were held on Saturdays.

Local community groups were still giving us a lesson in grassroots organising. We brought the Detroit Water Brigade to Cobh in Cork to give a presentation on their experiences of water shutoffs and water poverty, and on the visit we saw what could only be described as a military-style operation to keep water meters out of Cobh. There were only two entrances to the island of Cobh: one by road and one by boat. The Cobh Right2Water group had a 24-hour-watch system, and whenever they spotted a vehicle with an Irish Water contractor logo on it, the spotter would send a text message to the other activists and the entire community would mobilise to prevent the meters from entering the island. They had a horsebox for shelter and for tea and coffees. It was an impressive set up and a successful one.

The trade unions organised a number of promotional events and organised a stage for the protest on 10 December along with the printing of another 500,000 flyers, which were again distributed by the political, community and trade union activists. This time the event was held at lunchtime on a Wednesday in the middle of winter. We were optimistic but nervous. The Right2Water coordinating group were all eager to hear their own respective representatives on the stage. In the end, following much debate and differences of opinions, we ended up with 36 speakers or acts. The unions wanted a shorter event, but all the fragmented groups wanted their perspective heard and argued accordingly. People Before Profit argued in favour of a 24-hour protest. This would've been impossible to manage, and, given the weather on the day, it was lucky it wasn't attempted.

The event was wrapped up with the Rolling Tav Revue, a small group of traditional musicians from the west of Ireland, who had written a song in their kitchen (Kitchen Sessions) called 'No Privatisation, Irish Water Irish Nation'.

> There's no backing down, no concessions will do
> The people have spoken, you know what to do
> The time has come to stand and fight
> And not put up with the same oul shite
> We will strike, we will fight
> Water is a human right.

CAMPAIGN ISSUES

The issues we had with the Gardaí that day worried us. We knew the numbers would be big, and so did the Gardaí. So we agreed a release valve on the left-hand side of the stage which could be used by those with disabilities or those in distress. When the event began, the Gardaí reneged on their own proposals. Now, Des Fagan, Billy Wall and I were faced with a very tense situation in which children of eight to ten years of age were at the front of the demo and wanted to leave but couldn't. They had asked the Gardaí to leave via the left side of the stage but the Gardaí present refused. The children – some in wheelchairs – were deeply distressed. I subsequently came to the belief that the Gardaí were attempting to provoke the crowd. The stewards decided to lift the children over the barriers into the stage area and helped them to escape out the other side of the stage where a female Garda was only too happy to let them through to the exact same road the other Gardaí had blocked. She obviously didn't get the memo.

For weeks we had heard of a 'sinister fringe' and the *Irish Independent* went as far as to say, 'Senior gardai have said they are concerned that sinister dissidents had infiltrated water protest marches.'[4] One politician had the audacity to equate water protesters with ISIS.[5]

It's my belief that the provocation and commentary from politicians and the media was a deliberate attempt to divide the water movement. What frightened the establishment and government parties of Fine Gael and the Labour Party most was that the protesters weren't exclusively from working-class areas. On 1 November people from middle-class Dublin suburbs like Dalkey and Donnybrook turned up, and that worried them. What better way to deter middle- and upper-class protesters than to tell them they were marching next to members of the New IRA.

Over the previous weeks and months the Gardaí had also taken to helping the meter installers remove protesters in local areas. Oftentimes this was done in a very aggressive manner. Again, the mobilisation of the local grassroots became an inspiration. In November 2014 hundreds of women activists emerged wearing pink hi-vis vests. The first protest took place outside Coolock Garda Station where 200 women lined the streets in protest at the aggressive nature of the policing of water meter protests.

Audrey Clancy from the Edenmore Says No campaign in Dublin spoke to *Look Left* magazine at the time:

> The 'pink ladies' came about because during the course of men and women standing up against the corruption that's being enforced on the people daily, the Garda became violent towards the women. I was one of the women they were violent towards. I was pepper-sprayed. I was punched in the back at the GPO [General Post Office] for just standing there. And most recently at a water protest I was punched, which is now in the hands of the [Garda] Ombudsman.[6]

Another source of tension on the day of the December protest was Bríd Smith, now a TD, announcing the next Right2Water demonstration from the stage. She said it would be held on 31 January 2015. This was a surprise to the unions, who were funding almost all of the campaign. We had agreed a demonstration in the new year but no date had been set.

Up until this point, the coordinating committee had been approximately 15 people representing the unions and political parties, and almost all meetings had been held in Unite's offices on a weekly or fortnightly basis. Now, with regular mass protests and an unprecedented energy behind the movement, there was a clamour from different quarters to take ownership and control of the movement. The next coordinating meeting had more than 70 activists turn up at Unite's head office. The unions asked all participants to sign in and identify the organisation they were representing. One particular political party, People Before Profit, sent 32 representatives. This was quite obviously an attempt to bounce the unions into supporting the demonstration on 31 January. TDs and activists who hadn't turned up to a single organising meeting for the previous demonstrations were now demanding the unions weigh in with more financial support for demonstrations. If this campaign was going to have a future, it needed structure.

In January 2015, I drafted a blog explaining the structures as I saw them:

Right2Water has three main pillars, all of whom bring their own unique skills and attributes to the campaign:

- Political parties/Independent Representatives – bring political knowledge; an ability to raise issues in the Dail and Seanad, and have activists in communities all over Ireland.
- Trade Unions – bring organisational skills; are politically neutral; provide economic and political research; have activists in workplaces all over the country and bring financial assistance.
- Community groups – are the heart of the movement's resistance on the ground; have the ability to mobilise quickly and efficiently and provide a network of groups all over Ireland.

The combined potential of these three pillars is one of the reasons for the success of Right2Water so far. To date, the three pillars have worked closely together and with mutual respect for differences of opinions on tactics and strategies.

At this point some in the political pillar were demanding that Right2Water call for a boycott of water bills. The unions were adamant they supported the boycott tactic but that Right2Water was a campaign and not an organisation. We wanted to keep the coalition as broad as possible, and the best way to do that was to remain true to the founding principles of the campaign: 'All you need to be part of the campaign is to believe that water is a human right and that water charges should be abolished.'

Right2Water and its constituent parts had met to discuss the issue of tactics and had agreed we would support all peaceful means of resisting the imposition of water charges. The main tactics employed by those involved in the campaign were:

- Mass protests.
- Blocking the installation of water meters.
- The boycott of water bills and non-payment campaign.
- A political strategy for the next election.

This would be expanded soon afterwards to include political education and local events. Keeping the campaign broad enabled the grass roots of the movement to continue to adapt and utilise whatever tactics they wanted to adopt themselves.

Right2Water was trying to emphasise the importance of all tactics. The blocking of water meter installations was serving many purposes. It was costing Irish Water and the subcontractors a lot more than expected. It was also costing the state a small fortune in Gardaí overtime. It was also giving us a visible side to the campaign. The presence of social media meant many parts of the country saw a protest in Edenmore on Facebook and decided to replicate it in their own area.

The mass protests were giving people confidence and something to build towards. That confidence would have a reciprocal impact with the boycott campaign, which was another vitally important tactic. Some political parties, like the Anti-Austerity Alliance and People Before Profit, really pushed this tactic. We had to starve

Irish Water of revenue and make it unsustainable. The more non-payers, the more confidence the movement would have too.

When the first bills arrived, less than half of all households paid them. This created a confidence that we all knew would spread and strengthen the movement. John Tierney, Irish Water's CEO, referred to the 44.5 per cent of those who paid as a 'solid start'. Many within the water movement referred to the 44.5 per cent as fools, and some didn't want to be a fool a second or third time. By the fifth bill a year later, non-payment had increased to an estimated 73 per cent. The government was losing, and losing badly. The other important element of the boycott campaign was it enabled everyone to participate if they so wished. Not everyone could get to a mass demonstration, and a lot of people wouldn't or couldn't participate in the meter protests. But everyone could ignore their water bills if they had the confidence to do so.

The other side was spending much of their time attempting to divide the campaign. Government politicians and media outlets used a protest against Minister Joan Burton in Jobstown in South West Dublin to continue the ISIS/IRA/'sinister fringe' comparisons. The sensationalism of that particular protest continues to this day. Joan Burton, the leader of the Labour Party and Minister for Social Protection, who was imposing some of the harshest austerity ever seen in this country, was delayed in her car for a few hours by a sit-down protest.

The protest led to a 14-year-old, Jay Lester, being convicted of false imprisonment. The outcome was overturned on appeal. Paul Murphy TD and 19 others faced dawn raids by Gardaí who gave untruthful evidence under oath about what had happened on the day. While these events solidified the support of the die-hard protesters, there's no question it turned some people off the campaign.

RIGHT2CHANGE

Right2Water held another seven national demonstrations before the next general election. Arguably, however, the most impactful part of the campaign was about to begin. On 13 March 2015, Unite hosted the first of a number of political economy training sessions over two or three days for non-aligned community activists. Working-class people have great instincts when it comes to the economy and how it doesn't serve them. These political education courses tutored by Trademark Belfast help activists to join the dots and identify the problems caused by capitalism.

Political economy education was a key tactic of the global trade union movement in decades past. However, it had been relatively abandoned by trade unions in favour of more 'professional' courses which teach shop stewards how to utilise workers' rights legislation. While these training courses are important, they neglect the need for collective solutions to workers' problems and focus almost entirely on individualised solutions. When the economy collapsed in 2008, many workers had no idea what had happened. Some trade unions, like my own, Mandate, engaged Trademark Belfast to explain why retail workers were paying the debts of billionaires who had taken a gamble and lost. Now, dozens of activists who were protesting against the installation of water meters were learning the history of the privatisation agenda and identifying who the real enemy of their living standards were. It also built trust among the Says No activists and the unions, which was useful for the next phase of the campaign, the political strategy.

It was clear to the unions that there was much the three pillars of the campaign agreed on. This wasn't just about water. People were incensed by the state of the healthcare and housing systems. We called a conference to be held in the CWU offices on International Workers' Day, 1 May 2015, to see if we could develop a policy platform we could all agree on. The conference was limited to 200 people – 66 activists from each pillar.

Initially we proposed seven principles, including water, health, housing and education. We sent everyone away with a copy of the proposed political principles and asked all parties, trade unions and community groups and activists to give us feedback and observations on these policies. We reconvened in the CWU again on 13 June. It was a unique initiative which enabled everyone within the water movement to engage with the policy platform. By the end of the process we had ten policy principles: water, health, decent work, housing, debt justice, education, democracy, sustainable environment, equality and national resources.

Following the development of the principles, the unions engaged in a roadshow tour of Ireland. It took us to almost 30 locations from Letterkenny to Cobh, where we gave two presentations. One on water and the importance of continuing to fight privatisation. Another on the Right2Change platform and the need for Ireland's first progressive leftwing government. The events were successful, but we were faced with the same question over and over. 'How are you going to get the divided political groups to agree to work together?' It was a question we didn't have an answer to.

We called a meeting of the political pillar in Unite's offices and asked all political parties, 'Do you support the policy principles?' We also asked if the parties and independents would 'agree now to form a progressive Government based on the Right2Change principles if the numbers allow'. Finally, we asked, 'how will you work together to deliver this objective?'

We expected some resistance, but we were genuinely shocked when some parties did not endorse it. The unions at this stage were committed to running the campaign up to the next general election. This meant promoting those who had subscribed to the above questions. We printed and distributed 100,000 copies of a newspaper entitled *Right2Change* and, much like the flyers printed before every demonstration, we gave them to activists all over the country. The newspaper had articles from lots of different contributors, but in the centre was a supplement of each candidate in every constituency that was supporting the platform. One of the biggest failures of the political strategy was that, in our attempts to provide a platform that could unify the left, it left the door open for some whom I would describe as undesirables. Direct Democracy Ireland (DDI) contacted us to tell us they supported the principles and would be happy to work with others. We knew that many if not all of the activists within DDI were anti-repeal, that is, against repealing the Eighth Amendment, which banned abortion (see Chapter 4). This was a problem because the campaign principles included support for Repeal the Eighth. However, they insisted that if the Irish people voted to repeal the amendment they would support it. The principles also had strong support for refugees and asylum seekers. Many who now object to repeal and the provision of asylum demanded to be included in the platform and it was difficult to review the structure of the campaign to exclude them.

When the election was called for the beginning of 2016, we were ready. We called a national conference in the Mansion House in Dublin and a national demonstration the following week. While Right2Water and Right2Change weren't the only reasons for the seismic shift in the electoral outlook in Ireland, they played a big part. Labour lost 80 per cent of the 37 seats it had been elected with in 2011, dropping to only seven. Fine Gael lost 26 of the 76 it had won in 2011. The government lost 50 per cent of its vote. Almost 100 of the 158 seats were filled by candidates who had supported the anti-water charges platform, albeit the centre-right Fianna Fáil was one of those parties. This all led to a minority government with Fianna Fáil propping up a Fine Gael government, and Irish politics was changed forever. Water charges were abandoned, temporarily anyway, after a long, drawn-out debate.

When asked now about the legacy of the anti-water charges campaign, it's difficult to quantify. Tens of thousands were politicised, and that in itself is a success. Many saw how the actors of the state operated for the first time. How the establishment politicians, media and state forces, like the Gardaí, mobilised to a particular agenda against the interests of working-class people.

One positive outcome is that unions and progressive political forces were in place to prevent the movement from being co-opted by the far right. During several national demonstrations, the DDI, the National Citizens Movement and other far-right bodies attempted to get onto the platform. We stopped them. At the Kilkenny and Carlow roadshow events, members of the audience made racist comments and argued against taking refugees, with the usual 'let's look after our own first' jibe. We produced a slide for our PowerPoint presentation that killed off that argument, showing how much Ireland had spent on asylum seekers (€150 million) in previous years compared to tax cuts for top earners in the previous budget (€405 million). Had left-leaning trade unionists not been hosting these events, the direction of the campaign could have taken a drastically alternative route. We kept the far right off the pitch. Sadly, the abandonment of the campaign has left a vacuum they have happily filled since.

The limitations of the campaign became a frustration. Throughout the period of Right2Water's existence, nobody was working on the campaign full time. The bulk of the work on the union side was done by two or three trade union officials who also had their day jobs. It resulted in twelve-hour days for three years, and burnout on occasion. Had the trade union movement as a whole backed the campaign, instead of only five out of 48 trade unions, it is frightening to imagine the potential it could have had.

The political limitations also hamstrung us. There's a lot to be said for a proportional representation by single transferable vote electoral system, but it tends to fragment the left. We see constituencies where there might be two left-leaning seats running with up to seven or eight candidates. There's a very strong reluctance to put aside our 'angels dancing on the head of a pin' differences for the greater good, and that became very evident throughout Right2Water and Right2Change.

While there's virtually no remnants of the original Right2Water structures in place, the issue of water charges could erupt if any political party is stupid enough to attempt to bring back domestic water charges. The question now, though, is, who is there to show leadership should such a situation occur?

As Maude Barlow, author, activist and one of the world's greatest authorities on water, explained: 'The Irish system of paying for water and sanitation services through progressive taxation and non-domestic user fees, is an exemplary model of fair equitable and sustainable service delivery for the entire world.'[7]

That's worth fighting and uniting for.

NOTES

1. Willem Buiter, 'Water as an Asset Class Is Here', *Project Syndicate*, 16 December 2021, https://tinyurl.com/bde2d729 (all URLs last accessed August 2024).
2. Robert McNamara, 'Social Media Reacts Angrily to Joan Burton "Expensive Phones" Comment', *Irish Examiner*, 9 October 2014.
3. Juno McEnroe and Cormac O'Keeffe, 'Noonan Dismisses Water Levy Protests', *Irish Examiner*, 1 November 2014.
4. Conor Feehan, 'Convicted Dissident Was at Burton Protest', *Irish Independent*, 24 November 2014.

5. Steven Carroll and Marie O'Halloran, 'State Faces "Potential ISIS Situation" over Water Protests', *Irish Times*, 20 November 2014.
6. Aine Mannion, 'Women on the Frontline', *Look Left*, Issue 21, April 2015.
7. 'Water and the Illusion of Knowledge', Broadsheet.ie, 14 March 2018. www.broadsheet.ie/2018/03/14/water-and-the-illusion-of-knowledge/.

4

Abortion

Aileen O'Carroll and Máire Ní Chuagáin

On 25 May 2018, Irish citizens voted to remove the controversial Eighth Amendment to the Irish constitution, opening the way for the introduction of legislation allowing abortion in some circumstances.[1] Feminist and left groups had been campaigning for a liberalisation of abortion laws in Ireland from the 1980s onwards.[2] While the successful abortion rights campaigners drew upon this long history of working for Irish women's reproductive rights (including earlier groups) this was a new campaign. It differed from earlier generations both in terms of an explicit focus on changing the constitution to allow for greater access to abortion services (rather than accepting abortion only where there was a threat to the life of the mother), and its capacity to mobilise a greater number of activists, from a greater number of regions, and to include a wider diversity of organisations. This chapter will focus on strategies taken by one of the larger groups within the Irish pro-choice movement, the Abortion Rights Campaign (ARC), a grassroots all-volunteer group.

Social movements are a complex ecosystem of groups, institutions and individuals focused on bringing about change. The Irish movement to change the constitution combined both activist and institutional players.[3] Political organisations and NGOs were coordinated under the umbrella group *Coalition to Repeal the Eighth* founded in 2014.[4] In parallel, pro-choice lawyers, student unions and NGOs had been engaged in taking long running cases to international bodies challenging Irish restrictive laws.[5] In early 2018, as the long-awaited referendum was called, three groups – ARC, the Coalition to Repeal the Eighth, and the long-established National Women's Council of Ireland – formed Together for Yes, a short-lived umbrella organisation that, over four months, fought the referendum campaign. Together for Yes was led by women representatives from ARC, the National Women's Council of Ireland and the Coalition to Repeal the Eighth.

We focus on ARC as we believe the strategies this organisation implemented were innovative and new, and fundamentally key to the pro-choice movement's ultimate success. We will show how the non-hierarchical structure adopted by ARC allowed the organisation to achieve a scale of operations and capacity unseen previously. It will argue that the key to ARC's success was its ambition, both in terms of focusing on free, safe and legal abortion as a demand and on the referendum as a six-year goal. ARC's annual March for Choice became a marker of the growing support for reform in Ireland. From its earliest days, the organisation thought seriously about what would be needed to win a referendum through raising considerable funds and developing training resources for its members. Finally, while ARC may have been a necessary organisation, it is unlikely that it would have been sufficient on its own to achieve the change needed. ARC members understood that to ensure that their vision of stigma-free access to free, safe and legal abortion care was at the centre of the Irish pro-choice movement. It was important to develop working relationships and alliances with others within the movement.

TIPPING POINTS

This article will focus on the period from 2012, a pivotal date in the pro-choice movement. The year 2012 was to prove a year of tipping points, while some of what occurred then was planned, the scale and success of the movement that was to follow was also due to unpredictable forces, and in particular the tragic death of Savita Halappanavar.

In 2012, it was the twentieth anniversary of the X Case, in which a 14-year-old rape victim was prevented by the Irish police from leaving the country for an abortion in the UK. A court injunction forced their daughter to stay in Ireland. The girl's parents appealed against this injunction. The appeal ruling resulted in a court

judgment which would have allowed abortion in very limited circumstances to be introduced in Ireland, *if* legislation had been
introduced by government parties. In those intervening years all
the larger political parties, from right to left, with the exception
of Sinn Féin, had at some point been in power. Therefore, 2012
was a date which marked 20 years of inaction and delay, with no
legalisation in sight and little progress being made. As such, pro-
choice campaigners identified the date as a significant opportunity
to re-launch the call for a referendum.

The year 2012 was important for other reasons. Two years earlier,
in 2010, the EU Court of Human Rights had ruled that Ireland had
violated the European Convention of Human Rights by failing to
provide an accessible and effective procedure by which a woman
can establish whether she qualifies for a legal abortion under
current Irish law. As a result, the Irish government appointed an
export group to address the implications of this judgment. This
group was due to produce its report in 2012.

This led anti-choice campaigners to also identify 2012 as a crucial year. The activist group Youth Defence began an anti-abortion
billboard, poster and leaflet campaign in June. This campaign,
which featured graphic photographs, was widely seen as highly
offensive and resulted in an immediate and widespread backlash.[6]
Opposition to the publicity campaign was sudden and widespread. A Facebook page, 'Unlike Youth Defence I trust women
to decide their lives for themselves', became a focus for pro-choice
outrage and organisation. Grassroots organisers coalesced in July
2012 with the formation of a temporary umbrella group, the Irish
Choice Network.

Early in October 2012, the shocking news began to circulate
among activists that an Indian dentist living in the western city
of Galway had died in hospital of sepsis following a miscarriage.
Her request for an abortion once the miscarriage was evident
was refused. This death was to have a galvanising effect. The
Irish Choice Network soon became ARC – the main grassroots
organisation campaigning for a change of Irish abortion laws, and
specifically for the repeal of the Eighth Amendment – which is the
focus of this chapter.

CHANGING THE ORGANISATIONAL STRUCTURE

The structure of ARC aimed to be non-hierarchical from the outset and to empower all of its members to take an active role in the campaign. This is an approach which enabled ARC to build a strong, sustainable and empowered activist base. ARC's foundations were in anarchist organisation and the RAG (Revolutionary Anarcha-Feminist Group) magazine collective in particular, but it also attracted people from wider circles during its foundation stage. The early meetings of the Irish Choice Network involved women from anarchist groups and feminist groups, and women who were interested in abortion rights for a variety of reasons, including personal experience. The involvement of experienced activists in the early days of ARC meant that the organisation benefited from lessons learned during other campaigns, such as the environmental group Shell to Sea and the Dublin social centre Seomra Spraoi. New members employed in the NGO and Community and Voluntary sectors brought skills in key areas such as strategy, media and policy.

Early meetings focused on what organisational structure ARC would adopt – an indication that the first ARC members considered that how they organised internally would have an impact on the success of their campaign.[7] The structure outlined here is one which was developed over time and is based on three key

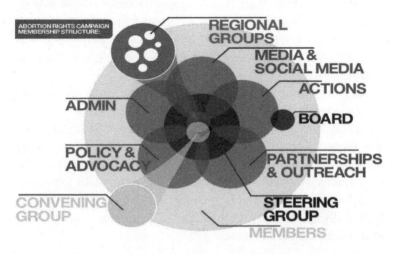

organisational elements: working groups, a steering group and a convening group.

ARC's organisational strategy can be described as one based on 'Grassroots, intersectional, non-hierarchical, community-based campaigning'.[8] This focus on non-hierarchical organising is in contrast with other Irish pro-choice organisations, such as the Coalition to Repeal the Eighth Amendment. The leadership of ARC changed annually, that of the Coalition remained the same throughout its existence. ARC aimed to mobilise activists. The Coalition's organising was (successfully) focused on building a consortium of civil society organisations under a constant leadership.[9]

The key structural element of ARC was its working groups. These groups changed over the years but included Policy and Advocacy, Partnerships and Outreach, Administration, Actions, Media and Social Media. All members were encouraged to be a member of a working group, and these groups drew from activists all over the country.

A steering group served as the decision-making body in between the annual conferences and was made up of representatives from each of the working groups. A convening group provided facilitation at meetings, ensured that the steering group met and could approve the spending of less than €150 and the adding of new members to the ARC online discussion forum. This group was elected at the annual members meeting and consisted of two co-convenors who shared responsibility, a treasurer, and a secretary. If issues were put to a vote at the steering group, the members of the convening group did not have a vote. Co-conveners were elected annually to serve for one year only. The purpose of these limitations on the co-conveners was to ensure that no one single individual was identified as the leader of ARC over the years.

In addition, ARC had regional groups and a board. The regional groups organised activity locally. ARC took the decision to register as a company and was therefore also required by law to have a board. Legal responsibility for ARC lay with the board.

The working groups gave ARC a task-orientated, rather than a membership management, focus. For instance, the Media and Social Media group was tasked with building and maintaining ARC's media presence, including the website and blog. The group developed posters, leaflets and postcards, responded to media requests, and trained spokespeople.

The benefit of decentralisation of decision-making processes into working groups was agility, in that the entire organisation didn't need to sign off on specific tasks. It also ensured that members were active in developing their own skills and capacities over time.

Having a set of core principles and values enabled the activist base to grow, attracting people from a wider spectrum of viewpoints and activist experience, while remaining true to the founding visions. Members were expected to be committed to ARC's principles from the moment of joining and there was an expectation that members would learn about the intersectionality of reproductive justice and all other forms of oppression.

In order to vote at the ARC AGM, members were expected to be active participants in ARC, which was defined as 'engaging in three ARC activities over the previous three months, at least one of which should be a meeting'.[10] Regular open meetings were held where the structure of ARC was outlined, and people were asked to join the working group they were most interested in. After attending two working group meetings, new members were added to the group's online discussion forum (Basecamp). Newer members were encouraged to get involved in social media, input into training and collaborate on policy documents.

The working group structure and the collective approach made it easy for newer members to get involved quickly. There was a high level of trust between members and a conscious effort not to gatekeep projects. It is inevitable that there will be a hierarchy of experience within any activist group, and as ARC grew these hierarchies of experience became more pronounced, however, ARC made deliberate efforts to empower new members to integrate themselves into decision making and operations.

ARC aimed to create an all-island campaign, building alliances with already established groups and, from 2016 onwards, supporting new regional groups to establish themselves became an increased focus. The Partnerships and Outreach working group led on this work, but other groups such as Policy and Advocacy, and Media and Social Media, also engaged with regional groups.

Regional groups could access funds for banners, flyers, and so on, and also received media support through media guidelines and design. Various workshops were available for all ARC groups, including Values Clarification training, media training and political engagements training.[11] As the number of groups expanded rapidly, a regional toolkit was developed by the Partnerships and Outreach group, which functioned as a step-by-step guide for new groups.[12] The toolkit contained information on running the first meeting, media and social media guidelines, how to organise non-hierarchical groups, and so on. To ensure that regional groups participated in decision-making processes, ARC held online meetings at a time when this was relatively unusual in activist circles. Funds raised were used to buy appropriate technology for those who needed it and for training on how to effectively run an online meeting.

Some local groups were operating in quite challenging circumstances, with many finding it difficult to book a room for an open meeting. Some groups had a handful of members who may have lived at opposite ends of the county, while others were more established and were focused around urban centres. Some groups involved experienced activists, while other groups were established by people who had never been active in a campaign before.

By building visibility and starting conversations at weekly information stalls in towns all over the country, local groups rebutted the anti-choice claim that abortion rights campaigners reflected the concerns of a liberal Dublin elite. They also highlighted the particular barriers faced by women travelling from rural areas.[13]

Supporting such a wide spectrum of groups effectively was challenging, when time and resources were limited and when the context of each group was so different. However, the network of local groups would prove to be a powerful asset as the referendum approached, as in many cases the structures and networks already existed for the formation of local canvassing groups. An ARC canvassing guide was developed in a ten-day period, as it became clear that a referendum was fast approaching. ARC activists provided early canvassing training and later the guide was adapted for use as the Together for Yes canvassing guide.[14]

By late 2017, when a referendum was around the corner, ARC membership had grown and included a wide cross section of experiences, knowledge and backgrounds. Some had joined ARC with radical politics, others became more radical through their involvement with ARC. Broadening the campaign and increasing in scale was necessary in terms of creating the political momentum for a referendum.

Although the legislative barriers in the north of the country were different from the south, women in both jurisdictions were denied access to abortion services. The northern organisations Alliance for Choice Belfast and Alliance for Choice Derry also held a yearly Rally for Choice. Both organisations attended each other's events, and ARC produced policy submissions on the provision of abortion north of the border.[15] The importance of this cross-border solidarity was in particular evidenced with the travel of volunteers from Alliance for Choice to canvass southern constituencies during the referendum.

CHANGING THE GOALPOSTS

The only avenue available for reform of abortion access was through a referendum; the first step had to be the removal of the Eighth Amendment from the constitution. From its establishment, ARC had three clear objectives: Legislate on X;[16] Repeal the Eighth; Free, Safe, Legal. From the outset, ARC was clear on its goals and its vision, and invested time in getting clarity on its objectives, vision and structures. It is unusual in campaigning to have a clear end point to work towards, a point at which you know whether you have won or not, but repealing the Eighth Amendment provided this laser focus for ARC. Where ARC differed from some other pro-choice groups was that it did not limit itself to repeal, it took a more explicit and overt pro-choice position with 'free, safe, legal'. While most activists in previous campaigns did support this position, it was often not felt that it was a position that could be won. Earlier generations of campaigners often focused on more limited demands.[17]

Holding on to this vision amidst criticism of it being too radical was key to ARC being able to maintain a cohesive approach towards their three objectives. ARC also identified the need to challenge stigma as one of its core aims, and including the word abortion in its title reflects how the organisation set out as it meant to continue. A mass movement could not be built while silence and stigma prevailed, so creating spaces where this could be challenged and where the issue could be brought out into the open was key.

In their 2016 election manifestos, despite growing pressure, neither Fianna Fáil nor Fine Gael would commit to holding a referendum to repeal the Eighth.[18] It was clear that political parties would have to be given no other option but to engage with the issue, and that the only way to do that was through public pressure. The annual March for Choice, organised by ARC and held around the International Day for Safe Abortion on 28 September, became a focal point for this pressure. The first March for Choice was held in 2012 with an attendance of approximately 2,500. This built to an estimated 40,000 at the 2017 March for Choice, which took place under the theme of 'Time to Act'.[19] The march was organised annually by ARC volunteers, who managed logistics, funding, stewarding, speakers, media and promotion and was attended by pro-choice groups, civil society organisations, trade unions and leftwing political parties, though the vast majority of attendees were unaligned to any group. Having an annual focal point where the groundswell was so visible was important for activists who may have felt isolated and exposed in their pro-choice activism, as well as for people who may have felt uncertain about how they could take action. This event became a central focus of ARC's campaigning work. It marked a change from many previous marches in that it wasn't a defensive response to an agenda set by others; rather, by aligning with an international day of action, it set a marker for the building of a more confident movement.[20]

As well as building political pressure through sheer numbers and visibility, the March for Choice also provided a space for local groups to connect with each other, and to foster a sense of unity and power across the movement. This mobilisation helped overcome the isolation experienced by regional groups. It also provides a focus for organisational and capacity building, through the funding of buses, breakfasts and accommodation for those attending.

Alongside the annual march, ARC groups around the country held regular information stalls, public meetings and awareness raising stunts to build the public profile of a pro-choice position and to make it clear to politicians how much support there was for a referendum. Within a few years, the main political parties were forced to adopt a stance on the Eighth Amendment. Events such as Strike for Repeal, which saw nationwide demonstrations and thousands of people blocking O'Connell bridge for several hours on International Women's Day 2017, also contributed to this momentum.

ARC had been building their finances in preparation for a referendum for several years, primarily through a partnership with the Workers Beer Company and through bucket collections at the March for Choice and fundraising events.[21] Initially, fundraising was undertaken by the Action Working Group, but, as the scale increased, in 2017 a new standalone fundraising working group was created. Fundraising enabled ARC to establish visibility through merchandise and advertising, and to provide the logistics needed to support increasing crowds at the March for Choice. It also meant that a funding basis was already in place for all of the requirements of a referendum campaign. While Together for Yes established its own, very effective, fundraising structures, there was significant value in having €200,000 raised by ARC members available from the early days of the campaign.

Because only state political parties had the power to call the referendum, the focus of pre-2018 campaigning was on building political pressure to force them to call a referendum. All political parties were involved in the Repeal campaign to some extent, mostly in the last four months leading up to the referendum itself, though in many cases activity was limited to personalities within political parties rather than the parties as a whole.

ARC recognised the importance of building alliances with the various groups within the pro-choice ecosystem. In some cases, alliances sought to draw on particular expertise and skill sets, as with Doctors for Choice and Lawyers for Choice. Often these alliances were built through working with groups on a shared project such as submissions to national and international bodies.[22]

In other instances alliances were formed to amplify the voices of those often sidelined in the wider debate on abortion rights, recognising that the Eighth Amendment impacted on everyone living in Ireland.[23] Now and then, it is often those representing political parties or who are in leadership positions who are given public platforms and campaigning events. ARC took a different position, prioritising instead the inclusion of many perspectives, ensuring that they shared their platforms with trans, disabled, migrant and traveller voices.[24]

ARC members emphasise that building relationships with similar international advocacy organisations was key in the earliest days. A two-day meeting organised by the Centre for Reproductive Rights (a global legal advocacy group) in October 2016, attended by a number of key pro-choice organisations, was described as a 'milestone'.[25] ARC members received media training from Catholics for Choice and also drew on resources from international bodies such as Ipas[26] and Inroads.[27] These international organisations gave ARC legitimacy in the eyes of other Irish political actors, money and support. The relationship raised the confidence level of ARC members and encouraged them to undertake more ambitious undertakings (for example, in raising a considerable fighting fund in the expectation that a referendum would be fought in the near future).

In some cases, alliances were built with those who did not hold a pro-choice position or share the non-hierarchical values of ARC and this was a more complicated process. Structurally ARC was positioned outside the NGO and political web of relationships. A simple example of this is that such groups were used to holding their meetings during working hours, which made it difficult for organisations based on volunteers to attend. These kinds of tensions came to the fore in late 2017 when it became obvious that a referendum would soon be called. Within the pro-choice ecosystem, many turned their minds to how the referendum could be won, and crucially what group or individual would lead the referendum campaign.

REFERENDUM POLITICS

The campaign to win a referendum is very different to the campaign to get a referendum. The former lasted a mere four months, the latter lasted years, arguably beginning in 1983 with the passing of the Eighth Amendment. The intention to hold a referendum was announced on the 29 January 2018; 17 weeks later the vote was held. It took eight weeks to establish and launch Together for Yes and nine weeks to run the campaign. The following section discusses some of the experiences and lessons of those final four months, but the exceptionalism of these months should be remembered.

As we have noted, some NGOs saw themselves as the natural leaders of the referendum campaign and did not envision ARC having a leading role in it. ARC members had to advocate for a seat at the table. ARC, however, had more money and a more extensive network of trained activists than other organisations. They had access to a suitable city centre office from which to run the referendum campaign. They had built strong international relationships and their various national and international submissions established their expertise in policy development. It was this organisational capacity which allowed them to enter the alliance which was to become Together for Yes from a position of strength. This strength was crucial. With it, ARC were able to ensure that ARC members were placed in the leadership of the referendum campaign.[28] ARC members were also able to influence aspects of the campaign's progress, for example, a code of conduct was developed by ARC members in which all groups agreed never to criticise or undermine each other in public (this is in contrast to the opposing side, which had a very public and destructive split).

In February 2018, following a robust debate, ARC members voted unanimously to join the umbrella group Together for Yes.[29] After six years of organising, there was a strong sense that the upcoming referendum was a turning point for abortion rights in Ireland. For many members, this involved a challenging process of balancing out personal values with those of a wider movement. Joining Together for Yes would entail a clear shift away from structures that sought to be non-hierarchical. Another key debate was the understanding that much of the messaging that had formed a core part of ARC's values, for example, ensuring the use of trans-inclusive language, would not be central to a mainstream campaign.

It is unknown whether ARC could have had the capacity to run the referendum campaign independently of an NGO-based campaign – it did not have the same access to the Irish corridors of power. History has shown that, here, making alliances was successful; the vote was won, but not without difficulty and compromise.

The referendum phase of the campaign differed in its goals and strategies: the previous six years had concentrated on capacity building and movement growth, the referendum campaign focused on ensuring that a majority of the population voted yes on the 25 May 2018. The following two examples show the differences in the two campaigns. Firstly the growth phase of the movement held intensive workshops for activists which directly addressed the right to choose and the stigmas attached to abortion. The referendum phase instead focused on those who occupied 'the middle ground', those who were either 'the soft yeses/soft nos', rolling out simplified messages which could be delivered at scale by canvassers, in leaflets, advertisements and televised debates. Secondly, the referendum campaign messaging often prioritised arguments in favour of abortion for medical reasons, particularly in cases where the foetus was not viable at the expense of the much more common experience of abortion where a pregnancy is not wanted.[30]

Once ARC subsumed its local groups into Together for Yes, local groups and activists were no longer involved in the direction of the campaign. Instead decisions on campaign strategy and messaging were taken by the three directors based in Dublin, often in necessarily secret circumstances.[31] Openness was replaced by silence and, in the fertile soils of a high-stakes, once-in-a genera-tion referendum, resentments and mistrust grew. Some feared that the compromises made for a mainstream binary campaign would change both the nature of the victory and the focus and future cohesion of the movement.

For the four months of the referendum campaign, many activists worked at a level which cannot be sustained over a longer period, and indeed many spoke of their exhaustion during this time and in the years following the campaign. Many activists experienced feelings of burnout, pressure, frustration, panic, anger, hurt and abandonment. These feelings were at times directed at the leadership and centralised staff of a now hierarchical campaign. In part this was due to a lack of support and under-resourcing of local canvassing groups, particularly in the early days of the referendum, when the campaign structures were being built and when materials were being ordered with limited finances. Communication was poor. Many groups were uncertain of how and when they would receive materials, and at times there was an absence of understanding by those in the Together for Yes headquarters of the challenges faced by groups campaigning in rural areas. In parallel, local groups were unaware that the majority of those directing the campaign in the campaign headquarters were also volunteers, with a relatively small number of paid staff working full time on the campaign.

The campaign hired a full-time campaign manager and communications manager. Three directors, along with four staff, from the National Women's Council of Ireland, who were seconded to the campaign, worked full time for Together for Yes from the start of the campaign in March. A larger number of volunteers worked part time, most joining later. One lesson derived from this experience is that it is essential for any campaign working through a grassroots network to develop a clear plan for communication channels and support for groups, as well as ensuring expectations are managed and adequate resourcing assigned. In its final review of the campaign, Together for Yes acknowledged they would have benefited from having more full-time staff, in particular to work with local campaigning groups.

The result of the referendum was a resounding 66.4 per cent in favour of yes, the long-fought battle to remove the Eighth Amendment from the constitution had been decisively won. The aftermath of the referendum victory poses many challenges for the pro-choice movement. As the group with the largest activist base, and one which was associated with intersectional and non-hierarchical organising, much of the post-referendum criticism was directed at ARC.

Some activists felt that too many compromises had been made in order to win a Yes vote. There was a feeling that, within the Together for Yes coalition, ARC had deviated too far from its free, safe, legal position, as the Together for Yes campaign prioritised arguments based on abortion for medical reasons, and that a more overtly pro-choice position would in fact have held with the middle ground. Some ARC members who voted for Together for Yes at the January ARC meeting later opposed Together for Yes's campaigning strategy, arguing that the voices of ARC allies, migrants, ethnic minorities, trans people and sex workers were silenced by a more conservative campaign. The Together for Yes *Campaign Guide to Messaging* includes the following section:

Who we are:
We are women. We are men. We are doctors. We are parents. We are grandparents. We are husbands. We are wives. We are trade unionists. We are students. We are workers. We are migrants. We are lawyers. We are rights activists. We are together for the women in Ireland who cannot be heard. We are Together for Yes.

However, the only other mention of migrants in the guide is a description of the Miss Y case in which a migrant woman was refused entry to the UK when she sought to travel for an abortion following rape. The second issue of the guide, issued a month before the referendum, includes a new section which outlines how migrant women were specifically affected by the prohibition on abortion.[32] In a statement written after the referendum, Migrants for Reproductive Justice described themselves as 'Women who saw Savita's image being used in the campaign, yet no women who looked like Savita taking centre-stage' and outline ways in which despite the referendum difficulty, the current legislation still stands in the way of abortion access to those who are vulnerable.[33]

Efforts were made within ARC to reflect on and learn from the lessons of the campaign and to acknowledge and address the criticisms, a blog post written a year after that referendum noted that 'by failing to include the voices of migrants, people of colour, and trans and non-binary people in the referendum campaign, the Abortion Rights Campaign (ARC) did not uphold our own values'.[34] Finding a path forward beyond the achievement of a significant and tangible milestone, while dealing with post-campaign burnout, was a difficult task, particularly for a volunteer-led organisation. ARC has continued to advocate for free, safe, legal and local abortion access since the referendum. For example, the annual March for Choice continued (with the exception of 2020 due to COVID-19 restrictions) at a reduced scale, ARC maintained its social media presence and made submissions relating to the legislation and subsequent legislative review.

However, since 2018, membership has dropped, many of the more experienced activists left the organisation and therefore capacity has greatly decreased. A combination of activist burnout, damaged alliances and divided opinions on campaign tactics and on the best way to acknowledge and address critiques in the movement has meant that, as of the time of writing, building on the victory of Repeal towards a wider cohesive movement on reproductive justice has not been possible. Free, safe, legal and local abortion access remains the cornerstone of ARC's organising but the answer to the post-repeal question of 'what next?' for the pro-choice movement remains unclear. The referendum campaign, and the movement as a whole, can be seen as primarily women led. ARC consisted mainly of women activists from its foundations onwards. Many male activists who had been involved in other campaigns were largely absent from ARC, and many of the men who became very active in ARC had no links to previous campaigns. While men may have been conscious of not taking up space in a women-led campaign, it is important to reflect on why more male allies were not present, especially during the years building up to the referendum. Did unconscious misogyny prevent men from working in a women-led campaign?

CONCLUSION: HOW TO CHANGE THE WORLD

This account benefits from post-hoc analysis and presents a cleaner and more simplified picture than the reality. The strategies outlined above developed over time following much discussion and experimentation. ARC did not have a clearly defined route map that would lead to success, they had a process which allowed them to learn by doing, and to adapt and move when opportunities allow. The non-hierarchical structure adopted by ARC allowed the organisation to diversify its activity, working in different spheres, while raising the skills and capacities of its members. An ambitious goal was set: a referendum within six years. This goal led

ARC to identify what it would need to win a referendum. It raised funds, developed training materials and built groups throughout the country. It attempted to influence the timing of the referendum through public displays of support for abortion, such as the annual March for Choice, pressure at international level via submissions to international investigations of Ireland, local pressure on politicians, and other public engagements. It raised the goalposts by rejecting narrow debates on limitations and instead it articulated the vision of 'free, safe, legal' abortion. Ireland is one of the first countries in the world which provides abortion via local GP services. ARC brought an intersectional frame to the reproductive movement by amplifying the voices of those often sidelined in the wider debate on abortion rights. It used its strength to ensure that those in the movement with more conservative politics were not able to dominate the movement as is so often the case. It could not predict that it would be successful – so much in politics is outside our control. However, ARC did put in place the strategies necessary to lead to success.

NOTES

1. You can request abortion in Ireland if you meet any one of the following criteria: pregnancy is less than 81 days (eleven weeks and four days) gestation, measured from your last menstrual period; pregnancy is causing a risk to your life; your pregnancy is causing a risk of serious harm to your physical health or mental health; the foetus has been diagnosed with a fatal condition and it will not survive more than 28 days after birth. Barriers to access, however, still remain, see www.abortionrightscampaign.ie/wp-content/uploads/2021/09/Too-Many-Barriers-Report_ARC1.pdf (all URLs last accessed August 2024).
2. Sinead Kennedy, '"#Repealthe8th": Ireland, Abortion Access and the Movement to Remove the Eighth Amendment', *Antropologia* 5, no. 2 (2018): 13–30.
3. Activist groups included the ARC, founded in 2012, Doctors for Choice, founded in 2001 and Terminations for Medical Reasons, founded in 2012; Parents for Choice coalesced around a Facebook page in 2014; Need Abortion Ireland began to provide illegal access to the abortion pill in August 2016; Strike for Repeal emerged in 2016 and Migrants and Ethnic Minorities for Reproductive Justice was founded in 2017. The Socialist Party established ROSA in 2013, and it operated as its vehicle to coordinate its pro-choice work.

4. Members of the Coalition to Repeal the Eighth included Amnesty, the Irish Family Planning Association, the Union of Students in Ireland, and others.

5. *D v Ireland* in the European Court of Human Rights in 2006; *A, B and C v Ireland* in the European Court of Human Rights in 2010; a complaint on behalf of Amanda Mellett before the UN Human Rights Committee in 2013. The UN Committee on the Elimination of all Forms of Discrimination against Women examined Ireland's abortion laws in 2017.

6. The Minister of Justice described posters in his constituency as 'obscene and insensitive', www.thejournal.ie/alan-shatter-abortion-posters-dublin-south-712382-Dec2012/.

7. ARC was supported in this task by Quality Matters, a non-profit organisation which provides training and facilitation services to community and voluntary sector groups.

8. Quote from ARC co-convener Sarah Monaghan, www.abortion rightscampaign.ie/irelands-result-had-given-hope-that-change-was-possible/.

9. There was overlap between the two groups. Ailbhe Smyth, the formidable convener of the Coalition was a member of ARC in the early days, before leaving to focus on building the Coalition. ARC as an organisation was a member of the Coalition. See press release announcing a meeting to build the Coalition which was held in Dublin in July 2014; Coalition to Repeal the Eighth. (2023) Coalition to Repeal the Eighth: 'Building a Coalition to Repeal the 8th Amendment' letter, Digital Repository of Ireland [Distributor], Digital Repository of Ireland [Depositing Institution], https://doi.org/10.7486/DRI.tm711n55m.

10. Abortion Rights Campaign. ARC Regional Groups Toolkit booklet, (2022) Digital Repository of Ireland [Distributor], Digital Repository of Ireland [Depositing Institution], https://doi.org/10.7486/DRI.cj8301105https://doi.org/10.7486/DRI.cj8301105, p. 11.

11. See, for example, the following archived at the Digital Repository of Ireland: ARC Election pack 2016, https://doi.org/10.7486/DRI.b564jj34r; 'Guide to Irish politics' factsheet, https://doi.org/10.7486/DRI.9s16dz982; Abortion Rights Campaign, 'Question your representative' flyer (2022), https://doi.org/10.7486/DRI.bv73rs22s, Abortion Rights Campaign, 'Responding to opposition' leaflet (2022), https://doi.org/10.7486/DRI.bn99q054r; Abortion Rights Campaign, 'Talk to your TD' flyer (2022), https://doi.org/10.7486/DRI.fq97nm586; Abortion Rights Campaign, 'What would a best practice model of abortion provision in Ireland look like?' leaflet (2022), https://doi.org/10.7486/DRI.c247tj9oh.

12. Abortion Rights Campaign, ARC Regional Groups Toolkit booklet (2022), https://doi.org/10.7486/DRI.cj8301105.

13. Abortion Rights Campaign, ARC Submission to Seanad Public Consultation Committee: A More Equitable Ireland for Travellers (2022), https://doi.org/10.7486/DRI.gh93wr30m.

14. See Together for Yes collection, Digital Repository of Ireland [Distributor], Digital Repository of Ireland [Depositing Institution], https://doi.org/10.7486/DRI.nv93js94h; Abortion Rights Campaign and Digital Repository of Ireland, Abortion Rights Campaign Collection (2022), Digital Repository of Ireland [Distributor], Digital Repository of Ireland [Depositing Institution], https://doi.org/10.7486/DRI.m9012j507.

15. Video of speech by Alliance for Choice at 2018 March for Choice, https://doi.org/10.7486/DRI.rb69b370b; ARC Submission to Northern Ireland Office consultation on abortion legislation, https://doi.org/10.7486/DRI.gx4219665; ARC Submission to UK Women and Equalities Committee: Abortion Law in Northern Ireland Inquiry (2022), https://doi.org/10.7486/DRI.gb19tz62f.

16. By this, they mean introduce legislation that would allow for abortion in the limited circumstances outlined by the courts following the X Case (that is, where there is a threat to the life of the mother including a threat to her health).

17. Sinead Kennedy, '"#Repealthe8th" Ireland, Abortion Access and the Movement to Remove the Eighth Amendment', Annuario di Antropologia 5, no. 2 (2018): 13–31; Cathie Doherty and Sinéad Redmond, 'The Radicalisation of a New Generation of Abortion Rights Activists', in Catherine Conlon, Sinead Kennedy and Aideen Quility (eds.), The Abortion Papers Ireland: Volume 2 (Cork: Cork University Press, 2015), pp. 270–4.

18. http://michaelpidgeon.com/manifestos/.

19. Mark Malone, Timelapse video of 2017 March for Choice (2022), Digital Repository of Ireland [Depositing Institution], https://doi.org/10.7486/DRI.pc28q8906.

20. For example, the X-Case march was held in response to a court injunction, other marches were held in advance of the 2002 referendum.

21. The Workers Beer Company runs bars at festivals and events. These are staffed by volunteers from campaigning groups, whose pay for the work they have done is given to the campaigns they represent. www.workersbeer.co.uk.

22. Examples of submissions: Abortion Rights Campaign and Abortion Support Network, ARC and ASN Submission to CERD Committee for Fifth to Ninth Periodic Reports of Ireland (2022), https://doi.org/10.7486/DRI.gt550d829; Abortion Rights Campaign, ARC Joint submission with the Sex Workers Alliance of Ireland (SWAI) and Sexual Rights Ireland (SRI) to the Universal Periodic Review of Ireland (2022), https://doi.org/10.7486/DRI.9k42c6301.

23. ARC worked with advocacy groups such as the Transgender Equality Network of Ireland (TENI) and SWAI.

24. For example, at the 2017 March for Choice, the following spoke: Emily Waszak for MERJ (Migrants and Ethnic Minorities for Reproductive Justice), https://doi.org/10.7486/DRI.p267mm385, Kate McGrew for the Sex Workers Alliance, https://doi.org/10.7486/DRI.nv93jt704, and trans-rights activist Matt Kennedy https://doi.org/10.7486/DRI.nso6hx86t.

25. Groups in attendance included ARC, the Coalition to Repeal the Eight, the National Women's Council of Ireland, Amnesty and the Irish Family Planning Association. Ailbhe Smyth, Gráinne Griffin and Orla O'Connor, *It's a Yes! How Together for Yes Repealed the Eighth and Transformed Irish Society* (Dublin: Open Press, 2019).

26. www.ipas.org/about-us/strategy/. Kate McGrew from the Sex Workers Alliance Abortion Rights Campaign, https://doi.org/10.7486/DRI. nv93jt704.

27. www.makeinroads.org.

28. Together for Yes was led by women representatives from ARC (Gráinne Griffin and Sarah Monaghan), the National Women's Council of Ireland (Orla O'Conner) and the Coalition to Repeal the Eighth (Ailbhe Smyth).

29. Abortion Rights Campaign, 'ARC Extraordinary General Meeting 2018 Agenda' (2022), https://doi.org/10.7486/DRI.g732t2798.

30. Katie Mishler, '"It's Most Peculiar That This Particular Story Doesn't Get Told": A Reproductive-Justice Analysis of Storytelling in the Repeal Campaign in Ireland, 2012–18', Éire-Ireland 56, nos. 3–4 (2021): 80–103, https://doi.org/10.1353/eir.2021.0016: Together for Yes, 'Together for Yes Factsheet: "Does abortion happen in Ireland?"' (2022), Digital Repository of Ireland [Depositing Institution], https://doi.org/10.7486/ DRI.hh646n70c; Together for Yes, Together for Yes Real Stories: Siobhán's Story (2022), Digital Repository of Ireland [Distributor], Digital Repository of Ireland [Depositing Institution], https://doi.org/10.7486/ DRI.fq97nm59g.

31. The campaign strategy is outlined in this report: Together for Yes, 'Together for Yes Report: Learning from the 2018 Together for Yes Campaign' (2023), Digital Repository of Ireland [Distributor], Digital Repository of Ireland [Depositing Institution], https://doi.org/10.7486/ DRI.0g35j7404.

32. Together for Yes, 'Together for Yes Brand Messaging Books – versions 1 and 2' (2023), p. 16 of the second guide, Digital Repository of Ireland [Distributor], Digital Repository of Ireland [Depositing Institution], https://doi.org/10.7486/DRI.jd47gp88f-3.

33. https://merjireland.org/index.php/2019/02/05/what-does-reproductive-justice-look-like-after-the-referendum-a-migrant-perspective/.

34. www.abortionrightscampaign.ie/where-we-are-together-we-are-strongest/.

5

Housing

Juliana Sassi, Seamus Farrell, Rosi Leonard
and Aisling Hedderman

In this chapter, we explore the twenty-first-century housing movement in Ireland. Shaped by a shifting housing structure, movements have built themselves, particularly since the 2008 global financial crisis, to challenge the insecurity and inequality of housing in Ireland and the explosive class tension between those who own and invest in property for profit and those who need a secure and affordable home and a community to live in. This has been marked by several tactical approaches from movements from above and below. In this introduction, we advance three key arguments to be developed in the later stages of the chapter.

Firstly, our argument is that, as in many countries, an important housing movement has emerged in Ireland after the global financial crisis. This movement consists of two main wings. One is a movement from above, whose focus has been on creating an institutional alternative to the economically liberal parties, Fianna Fáil and Fine Gael – and the Irish rich 'comprador' class who back them – and the other is a movement from below – focused on resisting the most acute points of housing impoverishment and creating flashpoints of resistance. The housing movement has been able to elevate the housing question to the mainstream and has created points of resistance and direct conflict within the housing system, making it a key point of tension in Irish society. We will primarily focus on the movement from below and how it has developed. Nonetheless, we understand that both wings of the movement are important and are more or less interconnected.

Secondly, the twenty-first century housing movement has been defined by flashpoint issues. These are places where the most intense conflict has arisen from 2008 to 2022 and where resist-ance on the ground has gathered the most force. They are: vacancy and dereliction, evictions and dispossession, and maintenance and mistreatment. Since 2020, with the creation of the Commu-nity Action Tenants Union (CATU), there has been an attempt to reconnect the response to flashpoint issues with longer-term com-munity building, which we will explore further on.

Finally, between 2008 and 2022, the housing movement on the ground (from below) has shifted and grown for two main addi-tional reasons. Between 2008 and 2014, direct-action tactics focused on vacancy (by anarchists) and mortgage evictions (by republicans) mostly remained as separate movements, dependent on previous generations of activists. From 2014 on, private tenants, particularly young families and unemployed young workers, Inter-national Protection Applicants[1] in Direct Provision[2] centres and homeless people in emergency accommodation emerged as a new working-class political subject drawing on and learning from past movements but then fusing and expanding direct action and com-munity organising tactics, escalating conflict points in the state and challenging more institutional progressive forces to take action.

In the next sections, we provide a background to the post-crash housing movement in Ireland. Then, we will discuss the period 2008–22 and identify the distinct groups and coalitions that emerged, as well as the tactics they deployed. We conclude by out-lining challenges to and the potential of the movement.

THE WORKING-CLASS HOUSING MOVEMENT IN IRELAND: NEW AND OLD STRUGGLES

In Ireland, the conflicts of the 1800s, often considered a politi-cal division between the British Empire and republicanism, were bound to questions of land and housing ownership in both rural and urban Ireland.[3] The late 1880s saw a period of intense defen-sive direct action against evictions, with groups such as the Land League and the Ladies Land League in the forefront of the struggle.

Following the land wars and independence, land was distributed to small and middling tenants, serving to protect the Irish state against radicalism, republicanism and communism.[4] In the twentieth century, rent strikes were dominant features of working-class resistance to repressive state policy. The 1930s, for example, saw a wave of action in Dublin, such as the York Street rent strikes of 1934 in response to overcrowding and unhealthy living conditions. It was led by tenants and supported by republican organisations such as the Republican Congress and militant unions under the banner of the Tenant's League.

In the 1960s, the Dublin Housing Action Committee and National Association of Tenants Organisation in the South of Ireland and Housing Action Groups and Civil Rights group in the North, organised rent strikes against slum conditions and evictions, involving thousands of tenants. In the North, rent strikes with an estimated 25,000 tenants were organised in September 1971 in opposition to internment.[5]

Many of these early struggles ensured housebuilding played a key role in the emergence of the Irish state, with large social housing building programmes taking place across the 1930s and into the 1960s. However, to a large degree many of these programmes retained a tiered housing structure, incentivising and prioritising the goal of home ownership for tenants over certain incomes. In many parts of Dublin with historically high proportions of state-built housing, contemporary struggles to maintain public housing and resist the loss of housing in the face of 'regeneration' has its own rich and deep history, as in the case of St. Michael's Estate in Dublin's south inner city.

Similarly, for decades Irish Travellers have challenged the Irish state for their own ability to travel, camp and access appropriate accommodation and services, and have often been met with some of the most violent instances of state repression for their actions, as in the case of the Cherry Orchard evictions in the 1960s.

THE CRISIS AND THE OLD NEW MOVEMENT (2008–14)

The Celtic Tiger period (1993 to 2006) saw a massive increase in the construction and delivery of housing, dominated by increasingly expensive mortgage-backed homes. The 2008 financial collapse saw house prices and housing stock decrease, salaries stagnate and unemployment rise while banks collapsed. To bail out the banks, the Irish state adopted austerity policies with substantial cuts to state spending and wages. This included cuts to investment in social housing by 72 per cent for ten years[6] as well as eliminating targeted supports such as those for lone parents and budgets for Traveller accommodation. Another shift was more general, moving from mortgage reliance to long-term rental solutions. This was facilitated by a range of measures to promote the private rental sector and attract investors, including sales of land and property to international (vulture) funds, mainly through the National Management Asset Agency (NAMA) as well as the introduction of the Real Estate Investment Trusts (REITs) tax regime in 2013 and schemes such as Build and Buy to Let.[7] In 2014, the Fine Gael–Labour government introduced the Housing Assistance Payment (HAP), a form of rent subsidy paid by the state directly to private landlords as a central method of housing provision. Thus, once receiving HAP, the tenant is removed from the social housing waiting list. Buoyed by these multiple factors and the near disappearance of new public housing after 2008, rents have rocketed. 2021 data from the Residential Tenancies Board revealed that half of tenants spend more than 30 per cent of net income on rent. In Dublin, the proportion of tenants paying more than 30 per cent of net income rises to 64 per cent.[8]

Resistance to state policies had been heavily contained in the 1990s and early 2000s by a model called social partnership, in which wage and social spending policies were agreed between the state, business, trade union and voluntary sectors. The result of such 'partnerships' was the de-politicisation of community activism and a shift 'towards "managerialism", direct service provision and top-down, professionalised approaches to the problems at hand, with an individualist, neo-liberal ideology'.[9] With the economy collapsed in 2008, the social partnership model was ripped up by the state and the business class in favour of open class conflict, the suppression of wages and cuts in social spending, including public or social housing. Progressive institutions, used to a seat at the table, were in disarray. However, possibilities for organised resistance and progressive change began to emerge around housing.

Opposition to austerity first coalesced around trade union anti-austerity mobilisation and the possibility of a Labour Party government. Labour's coalition with Fine Gael quickly became less promising, exemplified through some of its housing policies outlined above. Instead, smaller forms of resistance emerged around housing and community politics. The squatting of vacant buildings – long term to live in or in once-off actions such as Unlock NAMA, which occupied a vacant NAMA-owned building in Dublin's city centre in 2012 – is an important example of direct action in this period.[10] While squatting homes for residential use has a long history in Ireland, tactics of occupation such as Unlock NAMA took aim at new post-austerity institutions, including the demand to 'make NAMA properties available for social and community use'.

Large residential squats such as Grangegorman's Squat City, which also functioned as a social space in the city and which continued in various forms from 2013 to 2015, sparked the political imagination of a new generation of activists and offered a direct response to the growing issue of land hoarding and speculation in the capital.[11] Other tactics of the period included anti-rich walking tours and networks focused on naming and shaming the people who caused the financial crisis. The anti-globalisation activists of the early 2000s, including the anarchist organisation Workers Solidarity Movement and republican groups to the left of Sinn Féin, were a driving force to these efforts. Community activists and the voluntary sector, particularly coalescing around the Spectacle of Defiance and Hope, targeted the state's failure, with the collapse of Public Private Partnership agreements, to redevelop social housing blocks and its cuts to vital community services. The mortgage crisis was also taken up by left-leaning republican groups such as the 1916 societies, as well as by a more disenfranchised petty business class built around the Land League and New Land League.

The efforts to target housing inequality, the bank bailout and austerity measures following the financial crisis were largely disconnected. Nevertheless, they provided important points of resistance and provided the new housing movement in Ireland with a rich repertoire of new tactics.

THE SPARKS OF A NEW MOVEMENT (2014–16)

Rory Hearne and others describe housing movements as taking a different form after 2014.[12] Prior to 2014, housing movements emerged out of the pre-existing struggles of working-class communities during the Celtic Tiger years. Hearne and others argue that the character of these new housing groups was diverse, with many inspired by the direct-action campaign against water charges. Additionally, both anarchist and republican groups, as well as community activists, oriented their work towards housing and supported new political subjects, such as young unemployed tenants and families being pushed into homelessness, who organised to take action. This accelerated the move towards direct action which Mallon argues has been a growing tactic across Irish social movements over the past 20 years.[13]

However, unlike the successful water charges or the Repeal campaign, there was not one unifying demand connecting people fighting for housing. Resistance emerged at the margins first, in Direct Provision and emergency accommodation and was then taken up more widely.

In 2014, in protest at overcrowded and unhealthy living conditions and the treatment of people in the Direct Provision system more generally, residents of a Direct Provision centre in Kinsale blockaded themselves into the building and refused to allow staff to enter. Residents occupied the building for several days, placing national focus on the poor living conditions that residents faced – especially regarding independence, safety, overcrowding and access to decent food. The state responded by breaking residents up and moving them to different centres, underlining the threat that this organised action posed. In that same year, the Movement of Asylum Seekers in Ireland (MASI) was founded.

Much of the direct action from 2014 onwards in Dublin has centred around standards in emergency accommodation and lack of regulation of facilities, with private owners profiting heavily from the housing crisis.[14] This action has taken numerous forms, such as sit-ins, occupations of vacant buildings, and protests. The demands have at times been too specific or limited, but are of a clearly urgent nature. One group of residents who organised a sit-in at Dublin City Council in 2015 made the provision of food vouchers one of their key demands; due to being placed in private hotel bedrooms, the families could not cook any meals for their children. The group that helped to organise this sit-in was North Dublin Bay Housing Crisis Committee. Formed in 2014, this group was made up of people on the housing waiting list in Coolock, Darndale and Donaghmede – predominantly working-class suburban areas with large public housing estates. Most were mothers who had experienced being locked out of both the increasingly expensive private rental sector and the disappearing public housing system.

This group would become one of the founding members of the Irish Housing Network (IHN), established in 2015, as a network of grassroots groups which included soup kitchens, mutual aid groups, local housing action groups and broader action groups. The IHN centred direct action as a core principle and tactic, aiming to bring change and build class consciousness around emerging sites of housing conflict. It focused on responding to vacancy and homelessness but also mobilised around the conditions of private rental tenants, with an emphasis on stopping evictions. The IHN's work encompassed the three flashpoints we identify in this chapter.

The IHN's first collective direct action, the occupation of Dublin City Council buildings, was followed by the occupation of the Bolt Hostel, a former council homeless hostel on Bolton Street, in Dublin's north inner city. This action connected homelessness and vacancy as it aimed to draw attention to vacant buildings and resources which the council had at its disposal – despite rising homelessness and an apparent shortage of housing. The occupation lasted three weeks, bringing together locally based housing rights groups, republican groups such as An Spreach, and groups involved in running soup kitchens for the homeless. This action led to the creation of Dublin Central Housing Action which followed the model developed by North Dublin Bay Housing Crisis Committee of attempting to root itself in the local community and engaging in housing struggles on a local level.

In the same year, and also in Dublin's north inner city, a group of single mothers and families refused to leave an emergency accommodation facility on Mountjoy Street. Like an increasing number of people being made homeless in this period, all of these families were locked out of the private sector due to unaffordability. Preventing evictions and improving conditions at emergency accommodation sites – hotels, hostels and new family hubs – exploded in this period, and spurred on the use of direct action in private tenancies and social tenancies contexts. These experiences also helped cohere strategies to address the increasingly complex story of housing precarity in this period and the demand for immediate relief, and to transform housing into a secure public good through direct action.

At the same time, the Irish Congress of Trade Unions and the Labour Party's retreat from anti-austerity rhetoric, allied with the implementation of budget cuts, left a vacuum on the Irish centre-left to respond to social and economic inequality and discontent. Formed during the water charges campaign by a grouping of five trade unions led by Unite, a new 'movement from above' began to emerge that engaged the housing question. As Right2Water became Right2Change, large water demonstrations became broad progressive demonstrations, and a network of community activists were engaged to develop a policy platform that included housing and an electoral alliance of the left, modelled on Syriza in Greece, driven by the trade union wing, with some limited electoral success. A National Housing and Homeless Coalition was also formed, driven by People Before Profit, a leftwing socialist party, as well as trade union councils and smaller community organisations. Awareness raising and national demonstrations were the main toolkit of action, with some effort to bring together more radical grassroots groups and build a traditional left coalition framework.

ESCALATING DIRECT ACTIONS AND MOBILISATIONS (2016–19)

As the number of people becoming homeless continued to rise in late 2016 and the number of actions in response to poor housing conditions increased, a large housing action was undertaken, bringing together the movement from above and below – the Apollo House Occupation. This was a nine-storey office building occupied in the winter of 2016. Apollo House itself was owned by NAMA, which in 2009 had 21,500 assets in the form of buildings or land under its control. This occupation merged many of the flashpoints of the period, contrasting rising homelessness and standards in emergency accommodation with the widespread vacancy and dereliction in the city.[15] It was understood by the groups involved both as an emergency measure to house people who would otherwise be sleeping rough in Dublin over winter and as a direct challenge to the state's decision not to use the assets under its control to provide public housing and services. Over the course of the occupation, over 90 people who were otherwise sleeping rough stayed in the building, with over 200 volunteers divided into teams to provide day to day support in the form of cooking, logistics, medical care and helping to secure the building. Many more attended solidarity rallies outside the building, including a march to the Department of Finance demanding the re-allocation of NAMA's resources to address the crisis. This marked a scale of mass participation in direct action unprecedented in the struggle for housing in the preceding decade.

Apollo House was organised by a coalition called 'Home Sweet Home', which brought together the IHN with a collection of high-profile artists, NGOs, community groups and trade unionists. All 'partners' saw the value of engaging the flash point issues of vacancy and dereliction and tying it to the poor conditions that many homeless and precariously housed people were facing, as well as forcing a point of crisis by daring Irish government leaders to evict the groups during the Christmas season.

However, there were important differences of tactics and strategies – the artists and trade union wing sought to leverage the occupation to shift the narrative around housing, and achieve their demands from a Fine Gael housing ministry, while IHN activists, along with large numbers of volunteers – among them migrants organised in the Anti-Racism Network, members of soup runs, socialists and anarchists – aimed at building a form of mass civil disobedience that provided for immediate housing need and could be replicated and brought directly into communities, breaking the enforced housing scarcity.

Neither of the goals were fully realised, but the occupation escalated the level of conflict and pushed housing forward as a dominant social issue. Many of the individual groups within the IHN continued their focus on local housing issues through mutual aid and attempts to do more local organising and fight cases of mistreatment or eviction, build participation, and participate in campaigns for public housing. At the same time, new groups were emerging from below, notably through the increased engagement of students and migrants.

While the Housing and Homeless Coalition and Right2Change engaged in more static demonstrations and policy pressure on housing, Take Back the City started two years after Apollo House and became the next wave of large-scale direct actions around housing. Take Back the City shifted the target of the housing movement, taking the fight from the state and NAMA to private landlords and private market stakeholders involved in speculation. This was due in part to the growing number of private tenants becoming active in the housing movement and a rise in evictions – often the result of the state's mass sale of public assets through NAMA. The group Dublin Central Housing Action engaged in several mass anti-eviction actions between 2017 and 2019 in buildings in Dublin's inner city which had gone into receivership.

In 2018, Take Back the City occupations occurred across three city centre buildings in Dublin, with solidarity rallies and occupations occurring across other cities.[16] The first building was in a working-class area in Dublin's inner city, Summerhill, where months before 100 migrants from the Global South, mainly from Brazil, were evicted in a few days. Hundreds of doors were knocked to bind the neighbouring communities together around the actions. The intention was to carry out occupations that would move from one building to the next with an explicit goal of sparking off direct actions. The brutal eviction by private security backed by the Gardaí in Frederick Street created a backlash that escalated mobilisations, and sit-down protests followed.

Nevertheless, strategic differences emerged during the occupation, this time not between a movement from above and one from below but within an enlarged grassroots coalition. The main strategic orientations were: firstly, to engage in a series of continuous low-level direct actions against landlords, investors, corporate entities, councils and state bodies, coming mostly from the Dublin Renters Union and the student group Take Back Trinity; and, secondly, to turn towards and deepen a community organising model with a sense that the confrontational and propagandist direct-action style had shifted the narrative but not built a base in communities to fight back on a large enough scale to win. The second approach was supported mainly by community-based tenants groups.

NEW COMMUNITY AND TENANTS ORGANISING AND THE PANDEMIC (2020–22)

In the aftermath of these actions, the Community Action Tenants Union (CATU) was formed. CATU is a tenants group focused on building a deeper community approach to housing, direct action, and organising. This aim was not new, and for many this had been the desired outcome of the tactics and attempts towards mass participation seen throughout the preceding years. But it required the development of more sustainable organising models to achieve it. Ideas from Rank and File Trade Unionism, the concept of deep organising,[17] the history of the National Association of Tenants Organisations and newer tenants unions in the UK, such as ACORN and Living Rent, provided a theoretical and educational framework for collecting the radical fragments of occupations, anti-eviction and community action around poor conditions and rising rents into this model to build a radical, membership-based, community and tenants union. As a community union, CATU does not only campaign on issues that are 'explicitly housing related' but 'on all issues concerned with "social reproduction"; basically everything that goes into sustaining us so we can show up at work the next day', as Aaron Downey, former organiser with CATU, explained.[18]

In the first months of CATU's formation in 2020, those involved prepared for a long and slow build-up – door by door, street by street. Actions would escalate gradually, instead of focusing on specific emotive issues or flashpoints. COVID-19 suddenly changed this. The model of going door to door was suspended and the organisation had to face an unimaginable social, political and economic upheaval. However, fear of housing precarity and a renewed focus on mutual aid and solidarity during the pandemic contributed to a rapid growth in CATU membership from 30 to 300, 800 and then 1,500 members in two years, reaching 2,200 by 2023.

CATU's social composition has been plural, condensing in its core new and old oppressed groups. It is working class in nature, as it is formed by tenants of several types of landlords – 'mom-and-pop' landlords, corporate landlords, the state and banks. Nevertheless, other identities are also present within the class such as the LGBTQIA+, lone parents, people who are homeless, migrants, International Protection Applicants and refugees. For instance, today, at least 50 per cent of member defence cases[19] that CATU responds to are brought by migrant members, which is linked to migrants' reliance on the private rental sector, and their disproportionate vulnerability to exploitation and discrimination.[20]

Radical left political culture and social movement politics and a community-centred organising approach swirled together in the new union. They were both sources of tension over messaging and method, and sources of strength with the capacity to take rapid public action and build deeper organising bonds, with an education process that moves between the two. This has been more urgent since the rise of the far right, which has been blaming migrants for the housing crisis and systematically targeting International Protection Applicants in temporary accommodations.

In 2022, the Revolutionary Housing League (RHL) was formed by socialist republicans and other shades of anti-capitalistic militants. They have occupied several derelict properties to highlight vacancy and to provide shelter for the homeless. The RHL has continued to push the narrative around the housing crisis to the left through highlighting the various targets to be fought: government, private investors, developers in both public and private sectors and, increasingly, the far right. However, while CATU engages less in building an anti-capitalism narrative within the housing movement, it has been argued that the RHL is not building power within communities organically. A combination of both, and how to build it, is something to be advanced by the housing movement in Ireland.

CONCLUSION

There is a clear class and racial division in the provision of housing in Ireland, ranging from the institutionalisation of the marginalised and dispossessed at the bottom of society to social housing and temporary private rental, to single-family and multiple land and property holdings. In this chapter, we aimed to advance three main arguments to make sense of how the housing movement in Ireland has responded to it. In this conclusion, we revisit these arguments while also identifying contradictions and potentialities of the movement.

The first key point is that the period 2008–22 has seen the emergence of a housing movement with two main wings, movements from above and from below, with the latter creating flash points of resistance and bringing the 'housing crisis' to mainstream attention. However, although the housing question has entered mainstream debate, it means that housing has become a daily subject to complain about, which risks housing inequality and homelessness becoming naturalised. This is the problem if critique is not allied to practice and to the development of alternatives. In addition, housing inequality and deprivation can be instrumentalised by far-right groups to scapegoat vulnerable groups, such as they have been doing with migrants. This ultimately gives a way out to the government and the market-centred rationale if the housing crisis is not a political economic issue but is about demographics.

Moreover, the critique has been mainly around specific policies, while the role of the market and the state in a semi-peripheral European capitalist nation has not been fully articulated. This has led to incoherent strategies and short sighted and often merely reactive tactics. However, the balance of power and relationships between the institutional movements from above and from below could potentially change significantly due to shifts in electoral politics, such as the election of a Sinn Féin government.

This brings us to our second argument that an awareness of the limitations of once-off actions centred around flash point issues has led to the development of CATU, which aims to ground direct action within a community-based union structure. However, this itself is not without contradictions and challenges. For example, CATU's membership is organised on the basis of place-based communities in local branches, which creates challenges to connecting local and national issues – for instance, linking the union's national campaign for public housing with the specific problems and demands of local members, as well as providing for inter-branch exchange and support. Geographically, organising has also been more concentrated in Dublin; however, at the time of writing, CATU has hired union organisers in Cork and Ulster, and town-based organising in the midlands and west has emerged.

Our third and final argument is that the period 2008–22 has seen the development of a new working-class subject constituted by diverse groups who are exploited under the current housing system. This is manifest in CATU's aspiration to unify diverse working-class communities. However, while this aspiration exists, most CATU members remain white-settled, young, politically engaged, private rental sector tenants. This differs from previous Irish tenants unions, which primarily represented council tenants (reflecting the much greater proportion of public housing in the 1970s). Nonetheless, CATU has been growing in areas of high social housing concentration in Dublin, such as in Ballymun, Tallaght and Drimnagh.

Moreover, as the housing crisis grows, CATU's capacity to mobilise also grows. Its members have been evicted and replaced by processes of gentrification and regeneration and are now dispersed in multiple neighbourhoods and counties. This is an important feature of the geographies of the post-crash housing movement and, while potentially disruptive to local organising, is also contributing to the building of bridges between private and social housing tenants and settled Irish and migrants. Such expansion has also the potential to counter racism in communities where migrant members are organised, even though it can be a challenge for those to get involved once they feel – or are told – that they are not part of the community. However, we have seen that, by working together and highlighting contradictions in the housing system, trust and solidarity have the potential to build a pluralist working-class housing movement from below.

NOTES

1. Commonly known as asylum seekers.
2. Direct Provision was created in 1999 to receive and house International Protection Applicants as a provisional measure. International Protection Applicants were intended to stay there for no more than six months until the state provided them with suitable accommodation. However, 19.5 per cent have lived there for over three years and many others have lived there for up to nine years (Ronit Lentin, *Disavowing Incarceration: Asylum Archive Making Ireland's Direct Provision System Visible in Vukašin Nedeljković, Asylum Archive* (Ireland: Asylum Archive, 2018), pp. 3–10). The reality is that, as the housing crisis has worsened, those who gain their refugee status need to stay longer in Direct Provision because they have no place to move into, as social housing is insufficient and the private rental sector is unaffordable.
3. Terence Dooley, *The Land for the People: The Land Question in Independent Ireland* (Ireland: University College Dublin Press, 2004).
4. Conor McCabe, *Sins of the Father: Tracing the Decisions That Shaped the Irish Economy* (Dublin: The History Press, 2011).
5. Stewart Smyth, 'Housing Struggles in Ireland: A Historical Perspective', *Irish Marxist Review* 8, no. 24 (2019): 12–18.
6. Susanne Soederberg, 'Urban Displacements: Governing Surplus and Survival in Global Capitalism', *Journal of Australian Political Economy* 87 (2021): 5–19.
7. Valesca Lima, Rory Hearne and Mary P. Murphy, 'Housing Financialisation and the Creation of Homelessness in Ireland', *Housing Studies* 38, no. 9 (2022): 1–24.
8. Residential Tenancies Board, 'The RTB Publish Findings from Their Rental Sector Survey 2020 Reports', 14 July 2021, www.rtb.ie/about-rtb/news/the-rtb-publish-findings-from-their-rental-sector-survey-2020-reports (all URLs last accessed 23 August 2024).
9. Brian Mallon, 'A Radical Common Sense: On the Use of Direct Action in Dublin since 2014', *Interface: A Journal for and About Social Movements* 9, no. 1 (2017): 54.
10. 'NAMA v Unlock NAMA at the Great Strand Street Occupation', Indymedia, 2 February 2012, www.indymedia.ie/article/101309.
11. In 2016 the squat was violently evicted by a combination of Garda Siochana and private security, with several residents badly injured. Squat City was just one of many larger squats present in the city at that time, another notable building was the Barricade Inn, which occupied the Neary's Building on Parnell Street and ran a social space on its ground

floor as well as regular gigs and events. Despite its residents being evicted, much of the building remains empty at time of writing.

12. Rory Hearne, Cian O'Callaghan, Cesare Di Feliciantonio and Rob Kitchin, 'The Relational Articulation of Housing Crisis and Activism in Post-crash Dublin, Ireland', in Neil Gray (ed.), *Rent and Its discontents: A Century of Housing Struggle* (London: Rowman & Littlefield, 2018), pp. 153–68.

13. Mallon, 'A Radical Common Sense'.

14. Emergency accommodation is owned and managed by private enterprises and individuals while being funded by the state.

15. For a post-crash scenario of vacancy see Cian O'Callaghan, Mark Boyle and Rob Kitchin, 'Post-politics, Crisis, and Ireland's "Ghost Estates"', *Political Geography* 42 (2014): 121–33.

16. Juliana Sassi, 'Take Back the City: Building an Interracial Class Coalition to Fight for "Homes for All"', *Irish Journal of Sociology* 29, no. 1 (2021): 54–76.

17. Kim Moody, 'The Rank and File Strategy', *Jacobin*, 9 August 2019. Jane McAlevey, *No Shortcuts: Organizing for Power in the New Gilded Age* (Oxford: Oxford University Press, 2016).

18. Aaron Downey, 'Is There Power in a Union?', CATU, https://catuireland. org/is-there-power-in-a-union-part-1/.

19. In CATU's organising model, member defence is similar to the traditional labour union's workplace dispute – in which a member takes on their landlord for any reason of mistreatment or exploitation, such as rent increases, eviction, lack of maintenance, and so on, with the backing and active support of their local community branch and the wider membership.

20. Juliana Sassi, 'How Are Migrants Faring in the Irish Housing Crisis?' 4 November 2021, www.rte.ie/brainstorm/2021/1101/1257139-ireland-migrants-housing-crisis/.

PART II

Organisations

6

Trade Unions

Mary Muldowney

Irish trade unions entered the financial crisis in a weak position. The union movement had spent the previous 20 years focused on 'social partnership' agreements. These agreements ensured increasing pay but low levels of industrial disputes and gradually declining union density.

The subject of this chapter will be the reaction of the Irish trade union movement, mainly through the Irish Congress of Trade Unions (ICTU), to the 2008 global financial crisis, its aftermath and the initiatives that were taken to counter its impact on Irish workers. Following the crisis, as the implications of the austerity agenda that was introduced by the government emerged for workers, it even appeared for some time as if the trade union movement was finding a renewed ability to mobilise. Around a quarter of a million workers went on strike in November 2009 and hundreds of thousands were mobilised by trade union demonstrations. But by 2010, the union movement focused increasingly on securing pay agreements for its base in public sector employment. Outside the public sector, the trade unions have failed to reverse the continuous decline in private sector union density, although they have engaged in some broad-based campaigning and in winning some private sector industrial disputes. Both of which may offer some prospects for the future.

IRISH TRADE UNIONS BEFORE 2008: SOCIAL PARTNERSHIP AND DECLINING UNION DENSITY

The ICTU was founded in 1894, and in its years of existence no one in their right mind would ever have described it as a left organisation, but, in the final decades of the twentieth century, many Irish union leaders moved from the centre to the right, mainly accepting the business and political argument that free collective bargaining endangered future economic growth. The late 1980s saw an economic crisis accompanying growing employer hostility to trade union recognition, particularly among United States-owned companies that comprised the bulk of the foreign direct investment (FDI) on which the Irish economy was relying more and more.

From 1987 until the financial crisis, the Irish trade union movement had been worked through the ICTU in an industrial relations system known as 'social partnership', in which trade union leaders sat around a negotiating table with employers' federations, senior civil servants and delegates from community and voluntary sector organisations.[1] They reached a series of agreements on pay and taxation in return for industrial peace.[2] The government side also made commitments on a broad range of social policy objectives, particularly around the alleviation of gross inequality, poverty and social exclusion, although not all of these commitments were delivered.

Industrial peace was delivered by the social partnership agreements. In 1986, 309,198 days were lost to industrial disputes. By 2007, this had fallen to 6,038.[3]

During the era of social partnership, the economy boomed and employment grew quickly. Although union membership also grew by about 100,000, it did not keep pace with employment growth as unions found it difficult to break into many of the growing sectors of the economy. Union density fell from 46 per cent in 1994 to 30 per cent in 2007.

During the economic crisis that began in 2008, union density initially went up – rising to 32 per cent in 2010 – as union membership fell less rapidly than overall employment. But, from 2011 to 2016, both union membership and union density fell, with membership dropping from 498,000 to 416,000, while density fell more sharply from 32 per cent in 2011 to 23 per cent in 2016. In the most recent period, union membership has again risen – to 461,000 in 2018, but density has increased only slightly to 24 per cent, as overall employment has also grown. The Labour Force Survey figures show that union density is higher among women (27 per cent) than among men (21 per cent) and women account for 52.8 per cent of total ICTU membership in the Republic of Ireland.

Campaigners against social partnership on the left in the trade unions pointed out that the 22 years of having the ICTU at the negotiating table had steadily undermined the efficacy of the labour movement, especially with regard to weakening the traditional strength of the membership when it was exercised through their shop stewards, or workplace representatives. Local collective bargaining had been replaced for the most part by the centralised model that was the basis of the social partnership agreements. Legislation to limit the capacity to withdraw their labour had contributed to the pressure on workers to rely on paid officials to negotiate, with their only opportunity to object to poor deals coming when those deals were voted on, but only on a 'take it or leave it' basis.

THE 2008 CRISIS

In September 2008, the Republic of Ireland was the first country in the Eurozone to enter recession. This happened after 15 years of exceptional growth and fast economic development. During that period, Ireland had been the Eurozone's fastest growing economy and one of the richest countries in terms of GNP per capita.[4] But, in October 2008, the Fianna Fáil–Green Party coalition government had to admit that the country's banking system was tottering on the edge of complete breakdown.

As the extent of the catastrophe began to emerge, Fianna Fáil Minister for Finance Brian Lenihan announced that the 2009 budget would be brought forward from the usual launch in December to October 2008.

The measures adopted in the 2009 budget were blatantly focused on protecting those who were largely responsible for the disaster, by taking the costs of the recovery measures from low-paid workers and social welfare recipients.

In July 2008 the unemployment rate in the country had been 6.5 per cent but by the following July it had risen to 12.5 per cent. Unemployment would continue to rise, reaching a high of 15.1 per cent in February 2012.[5]

Despite widespread warnings about the likely impact on the low paid and vulnerable, the Fianna Fáil–Green Party government guaranteed all banking deposits and liabilities, which in effect became sovereign debt. The government debt-to-GDP ratio increased from a relatively modest 24 per cent in 2007 to 123 per cent in 2013, while the deficit-to-GDP ratio increased from a small surplus in 2007 to a deficit of 32.4 per cent in 2010 – the largest increase among the European Union's (EU) 27 countries.[6]

The ICTU had to respond to this on behalf of their members more militantly than they had done for decades, being urged to do so by affiliates such as the MANDATE union, representing low-paid retail workers for the most part, and Unite the Union. However, their ability to do so had been undermined by the years of declining density and declining militancy during the partnership era.

ICTU'S SEARCH FOR AN ALTERNATIVE TO AUSTERITY

On 21 February 2009, a demonstration organised by ICTU had brought more than 100,000 people onto the streets of Dublin in protest about the impact of the austerity measures imposed on ordinary workers, especially the low paid and those engaged in precarious work.[7]

Following the February 2009 demonstration, when the participants made it clear that they were fully aware of where the blame lay for the situation, ICTU published a document called *Shifting the Burden*, in which they condemned the government's strategy for recovery. They noted that the budget took just €73 million from millionaires but over €760 million from social welfare recipients, between cuts and additional taxation. The document cited an open letter to the *Irish Times* from 28 economic experts, who warned that the proposed measures would make things much worse, as all the wrong options had been pursued. It also pointed to the contradictions in the government's claims that wage cuts were essential to ensure competitiveness internationally, quoting the National Competitiveness Council (NCC), the official advisory body, to show that the real agenda here was attacking the conditions of those who could least afford cuts.[8]

ICTU tried to press for an alternative approach, which they described as a social solidarity pact, which would include investment in job creation schemes and education and training. It was not a particularly radical approach as it would still mean sacrifices from those least able to contribute to the recovery, but it was effectively opposed by elements in the government and the media who insisted that public sector workers were being paid too much and had privileged conditions unavailable to private sector workers, and that cutting them down to size offered a roadmap to reducing the country's debt.

Despite the failure of the ICTU to attract political or popular support for their suggested alternatives to austerity measures, several unions balloted for industrial action, hoping to emulate the resistance in European countries where mass protests had been taking place. The largest union, Services, Industrial, Professional and Technical Union (SIPTU), won a majority in favour of widespread strike activity. IMPACT, the largest public service union (now called Fórsa), did not secure the necessary two-thirds majority that was needed to sanction a strike. Other unions did not ballot at all and argued that the ballot result in IMPACT suggested that there would not be support, even in the public sector, for a national strike. However, there was a one-day national strike by public sector workers on 24 November 2009. Around 250,000 workers went on strike. Thousands of workers picketed around the country; schools were closed and there was widespread disruption to many services, although public transport ran normally. Emergency cover was in place in essential health services, though strike exemptions were granted to key areas, including palliative and intensive care. There were messages of support for the strikes from the various Garda (police) representative bodies, who were legally prohibited from striking.

Follow-up strikes proposed for December 2009 did not take place because the public sector unions became involved in the talks with the government that eventually resulted in the Croke Park Agreement that was signed in June 2010.[9] In the course of the discussions and in publicising the terms of the agreement, senior members of the government, including the Taoiseach and the Minister for Finance, repeatedly referred to the privileged position of public sector workers, who they claimed benefited from better conditions than their private sector counterparts. This narrative was also propagated by the media, usually without analysis of the claims.

Some private sector unions were intimidated by the fear that employers would use the 1990 Industrial Relations Act to argue that a strike unconnected to a legitimate trade dispute would be illegal and the penalties (mainly large fines) could be catastrophic for organisations already struggling financially. They did not get involved in the public sector unions' initiatives.

In December 2009, the private sector employer's federation (IBEC) withdrew from the social partnership terms. Danny McCoy, IBEC CEO, stated 'we are entering a period of enterprise-level bargaining in unionised employments'.[10] This effectively led to the development of two separate systems of collective bargaining on pay, one for the private sector and a separate one specific to the public sector.

THE CROKE PARK AGREEMENT

The government invited members of the ICTU Public Services Committee (PSC) and employers to enter talks under the auspices of the Labour Relations Commission (LRC), to be conducted in the Croke Park Conference Centre in Dublin. The Garda and Defence Forces representative associations, who had been generally excluded from social partnership negotiations, were also included in the invitation.

At the time, workers in the public sector accounted for roughly one-fifth of the total Irish workforce. The government's basic requirement was for the agreement to deliver cuts in the number of staff and the resources they were allocated without affecting the quality of public service being delivered and ideally, for supporters of the agreement, for the latter to be improved. This objective was in line with the determination to get the budget deficit below 3 per cent of gross domestic product by 2014 as demanded by the Troika.

The Croke Park Agreement was negotiated while the Fianna Fáil–Green Party coalition was still in government, but it had broad cross-party support. It was signed off in June 2010 and the new

Fine Gael–Labour coalition took over in 2011. While the Labour Party said they were determined that the Croke Park Agreement would be honoured, senior Fine Gael figures like then Transport Minister Leo Varadkar were saying it did not go far enough and further cuts needed to be implemented.

THE TROIKA, THE ECONOMIC ADJUSTMENT PROGRAMME AND A CHANGE OF GOVERNMENT

As the economic crisis continued to unfold, in late 2010 the Fianna Fáil–Green Party coalition, faced with a large deficit, turned to the Troika of the European Central Bank (ECB), the International Monetary Fund (IMF) and the EU for a 'bailout'. This 'bailout', officially named the Economic Adjustment Programme (EAP), was to be paid for by ordinary citizens, who had not benefited from the reckless gambling that precipitated the disaster.

In 2011 the first post-crash general election ushered in a coalition of Fine Gael and Labour. The unions were afraid that anger over austerity and Fianna Fáil's role in imposing austerity would result in the centre-right Fine Gael being able to form a one-party government and it was agreed that the ICTU would throw their support behind Labour Party candidates. In the event, Fine Gael did not win enough seats to govern on their own and Labour doubled their vote from the previous election, suggesting that the rhetoric of their manifesto was connecting with voters, whose expectations had been raised that Labour in government would challenge the influence of the Troika.

SIPTU had a formal affiliation to the Labour Party at that time (it was ended in 2017) and the union's members were urged to vote Labour as a means of putting a brake on Fine Gael's rightwing propensities. David Begg, general secretary of the ICTU, said at the time that unions could not afford to undermine the only party which was likely to challenge austerity measures and the demands of the Troika. Labour's rhetoric was promising but their elected representatives failed to prevent the imposition of Fine Gael's procyclical fiscal policy, which emulated the neoliberal approach of the ideologues in the ECB and the EU.[11]

Some unions were critical of what was seen as Labour's timidity as the minority partner in the coalition. This perception was not improved when, in 2012, several employers mounted legal challenges to the Registered Employment Agreements (REAs) and Joint Labour Committees (JLCs), which had provided a mechanism for decades for protecting the floor of rights for low-paid workers. Unions representing such workers lobbied for legislation to copper fasten the previous arrangements and the government enacted the Industrial Relations (Amendment) Act 2012. However, in response to a further legal challenge from a group of employers, the Supreme Court ruled that REAs and JLCs were unconstitutional, and it was some years before the situation was resolved in favour of the workers employed in the relevant sectors.

The Troika's insistence on labour market reform was also reflected in the changes to the architecture of the industrial relations system in Ireland. The five existing Irish workplace relations bodies were replaced by a new two-tier structure: a new Workplace Relations Commission[12] (WRC) and an expanded Labour Court remit in the REA/JLC sectors.[13]

CROKE PARK TWO

The Croke Park Agreement was supposed to last until December 2013, but additional demands from the Troika in 2012 meant that the Irish government was soon looking for an extra €1 billion in payroll savings from the public sector, giving rise to a new round of negotiations. The objective of new negotiations between the PSC and the Department of Public Expenditure and Reform (DPER) was to revise the original Croke Park Agreement. The PSC represented a total of 290,000 public servants, spread over roughly 20 unions. Separate talks were held between government officials and representatives of the defence forces and the police.

The government proposals put forward in 'Croke Park Two' were rejected by a majority of public service unions and by a large majority of members, including SIPTU this time. Fearing the rejection would be followed by industrial action on a wide scale, the government engaged with individual public service unions to negotiate a series of bilateral agreements, rather than the collective agreement that had been the basis of the Croke Park Agreement. The resulting deal was known as the Public Service Stability Agreement 2013–2016, or the Haddington Road Agreement, as the talks took place in Tom Johnson House on Haddington Road in Dublin, the home of the Labour Court and the LRC.

At this point, the government amended the Financial Emergency Measures in the Public Interest (FEMPI) Act to give the government power to unilaterally cut wages and impose other changes from 1 July 2013. The government favoured more stick than carrot and announced that pay cuts for public servants earning between €65,000 and €100,000 a year would be permanent, when previous proposals had offered the possibility of pay cuts being restored once the financial crisis was over. The Croke Park Agreement's job protection guarantee and the limit it placed on how far away from a current job a redeployed worker could be expected to travel would be taken away as well.[14]

Ultimately, concessions were made offering a quicker return to pre-July 2013 pay rates for staff earning between €65,000 and €100,000. Double-time premium payments, valuable for nurses and police officers, would be retained for staff rostered to work on Sundays. Concessions were also made on matters such as the payment of increments, overtime, working time, contracts, work sharing and flexitime working. Meanwhile, no worker earning below €65,000 a year would have their pay cut, although they might have to accept a short delay in payment of their annual rise.[15]

All but three of the 20 PSC unions voted for the revised deal that went 'live' on 1 July 2013. The exceptions were education sector unions, the Teachers' Union of Ireland (TUI), the Association of Secondary Teachers in Ireland (ASTI) and the Irish Federation of University Teachers (IFUT). Large majorities in favour were recorded in most ballots, with 76 per cent of the members of SIPTU giving their approval compared to the 53.7 per cent vote against Croke Park Two. The Civil and Public Services Union (CPSU) national executive recommended a 'No' vote to its members but provided them with detailed examples of how enforced wage cuts through emergency legislation would affect their pay and conditions. CPSU members backed the Haddington Road deal.

Unite the Union also recommended rejection, and its 6,000 public sector members voted against acceptance of the agreement. However, following legal advice, Unite also gave detailed examples of how the FEMPI would affect workers and a second ballot overturned the initial response. IFUT and the TUI also reversed their votes. The ASTI maintained their opposition to the agreement, citing their members' opposition to the negative impact the education cuts were having on children's education. Following further negotiations, the ASTI members voted in December 2013 to accept the terms of the Haddington Road Agreement, and they were given refunds of the additional pay that had been taken from them under FEMPI rules.

BROAD-BASED CAMPAIGNS

While the Croke Park and Haddington Road public sector pay agreements dominated the work of the trade union movement after 2009, they were not the sole focus of the union movement. Follow-up demonstrations to the February 2009 street protests were organised with another mainly public sector march in November 2010, the 'March for a Better Way' and a 'Day of Action against Austerity' in February 2013.

The union movement also participated in some broad-based campaigns. Of particular significance were the movements against the water tax and around housing.

In 2011, the Fine Gael–Labour coalition announced the introduction of a local property tax, to be levied on all residential properties. A national group to oppose this tax named the Campaign Against Household and Water Taxes (CAHWT) was launched. Although, the CAHWT had been supported by prominent leftwing political parties, the campaign received no formal affiliation from trade unions and it was defeated in 2013.[16]

The following year, in 2014, it became clear that the government intended to reintroduce water charges. Very similar charges had been roundly rejected by ordinary people in the 1990s. Trade union involvement in this campaign was much greater than in the campaign against household tax. A trade union led campaign called Right2Water was founded by MANDATE along with the

Communication Workers Union (CWU), the CPSU, OPATSI and Unite.[17] The campaign succeeded in forcing the government to back off as it became obvious that the strength of feeling about the proposal was likely to impact on voters' choices at the next general election.

In 2018, the trade union led Raise the Roof campaign was launched to challenge successive governments' inaction on the housing crisis in Ireland and to insert the right to a home in the constitution, although this campaign has failed to gain as much traction as Right2Water.[18]

THE TRADE UNION MOVEMENT AFTER THE TROIKA

On 15 December 2013, Ireland exited the Troika's EAP, although it will be several more years before the post-programme surveillance ends. The vast majority of policy conditions under the programme were met, thereby restoring investor confidence to the satisfaction of the EU and the ECB. The surveillance will continue until at least 75 per cent of the financial assistance received has been repaid. This is to be around 2031.[19]

Between the exit of the bailout and the calamitous impact of the COVID-19 pandemic, with the Troika out of the country and an improved economic situation, unions were facing a more favourable environment for industrial victories. Teachers and nurses used strike action to challenge the two-tier pay arrangements which had been agreed to by the union leadership in the course of the financial crisis, in 2016, 2019 and 2020, with clear public support for their demands. In 2015 and 2018, retail workers in a number of supermarket chains also took industrial action in protest about their pay and conditions at a time of high profits for their employers. In 2020, when the Debenhams department store announced that their branches in Ireland would be closing, without arranging for redundancy payments to their employees, the workers went on a prolonged strike to prevent the liquidation of assets in support of their demand for enhanced settlements. They were also supported by the public. But the strike finally ended after 406 days when the workers accepted a government-brokered offer by the company which they had previously rejected. The shop stewards blamed the government for using the Gardaí to facilitate the removal of goods for sale by the liquidator, rather than protecting the legal entitlements of the workers.

An important success was achieved in 2018 with an international collaboration between Fórsa and unions in other countries when the low-cost and notoriously anti-union airline Ryanair was compelled to grant union recognition to representatives of pilots and cabin crew. This victory and the methods used to achieve it should surely indicate the potential for pressure on an unpopular government to introduce an enforceable legal framework to support union representation in workplaces. Despite workers' constitutional right to join a union in Ireland, under Irish law employers can still refuse to recognise or negotiate with their employees' unions.

The ICTU decided to lobby the EU to introduce protection for collective bargaining rights in Ireland. The 2022 EU Directive on Adequate Minimum Wages includes provisions to improve collective bargaining in member states like Ireland where bargaining coverage is less than 80 per cent. However, while the announcement of this Directive was welcomed by the trade unions in Ireland, so far, they have not shown any indication that they will mobilise the membership to demand the change. One of the reasons for this apparent timidity might well be the difficulty of recruiting young people to union membership, especially in the multinational companies on which the Irish economy is very reliant. FDI-dominated industrial sectors have very low unionisation rates. This problem is two-fold: not only does it mean that unions' financial resources are negatively impacted but this sector is also one that attracts younger, more highly educated and skilled workers, whose exclusion from union membership is a weakness for the movement.

The result of the 2020 general election indicated the strong support for a movement away from the mainstream parties who had dominated the first 100 years of an independent Irish state – Fianna Fáil, Fine Gael and the Labour Party. Labour was never strong, and the party's failure to challenge Fine Gael policies in coalition saw their vote decimated. While Sinn Féin were the clear winners in terms of votes cast, they had no natural partners, which allowed Fianna Fáil, Fine Gael and the Green Party to form a government.

As mentioned above, SIPTU ceased its organisational affiliation with the Labour Party in 2017 and the union's political fund can now be used to support any union-related candidates, not just those running for Labour. So far, this has not benefited radical left candidates, who have not been notable for working closely with trade unions. Since many union leaders still see social partnership in a positive light, this is unlikely to change the perception of them in the eyes of leftwing groups who focus on grass roots level mobilisation in industrial relations.

Since Irish voters are leaning towards the centre-left in recent years, it may be that the trade unions' political involvement will follow this trend towards support for Sinn Féin, who have clearly been recognising the potential of harnessing the country's dissatisfaction with the rightwing parties. However, Sinn Féin's record in government in Northern Ireland does not promise any great hope for workerist policies in the Republic, other than in gaining them votes.

CONCLUSION AND FUTURE PROSPECTS
FOR TRADE UNIONS IN IRELAND

After the scale of the 2008 financial crisis emerged and social partnership in Ireland collapsed in the following year, the initial response of the trade union movement (indicated primarily by ICTU's approach as the representative body) was to engage in industrial strife and to protest vigorously about the impact of the austerity measures favoured by the Irish government and the EU. In the face of strict surveillance after the so-called 'bailout' by the EU, the ECB and the IMF, the Irish government imposed most of the recovery mechanisms on the low paid and on social welfare recipients. Rather than challenge this by mobilising the still large numbers of union members, the union leadership reverted to concession bargaining and reliance on influence rather than pressure. This approach has had some limited successes, but union density and membership has only recovered very marginally. Union militancy has reverted to pre-recessionary levels, with only 5,256 days lost to industrial action in 2022.

Many unions have now adopted an organising rather than a service model which has meant a greater focus on campaigning in recent years, especially on such crucial issues as the housing crisis and public ownership of vital resources and services. These social movement campaigns seem to be having a positive effect in that recent surveys show that public perceptions of unions in Ireland are above the EU average, especially among young people.

The relatively static positioning of radical left parties in Irish politics suggests that trade union leaders will not be motivated to make any move in the direction of alliances with such groups, at least in the foreseeable future. The rise of Sinn Féin and its more flexible ideology may appeal but does not address the challenge to unionise multinational corporations.[20] Collaboration with social movement actors and recognition that trade unions can play a vital role in tackling problems that are not confined to workplaces point to what looks like an effective approach to restoring confidence in unions and actually achieving important change.

NOTES

1. The community and voluntary bodies were not involved in the pay and taxation bargaining but did participate in the policy discussions.
2. The seven social partnership programmes from this period were: 1987–1990 – *Programme for National Recovery* (PNR); 1991–94 – *Programme for Economic and Social Progress* (PESP); 1994–96 – *Programme for Competitiveness and Work* (PCW); 1997–2000 – *Partnership 2000, for Inclusion, Employment and Competitiveness* (P2000); 2000–2003 – *Programme for Prosperity and Fairness* (PPF); 2003–2005 – *Sustaining Progress* (SP); 2006–2009 – *Towards 2016* (T2016).
3. Central Statistics Office, Industrial Disputes, https://data.cso.ie/table/IDA01 (last accessed 28 June 2024).
4. Eurostat, Total Population (national accounts) (NPTD); gross national income at current market prices per head of population (HVGNP), AMECO (annual macro-economic database) https://ec.europa.eu/eurostat (last accessed 26 February 2024).
5. Central Statistics Office, Seasonally Adjusted Standardised Unemployment Rates (SUR), https://data.cso.ie/table/LRM03 (last accessed 28 June 2024).
6. John Geary, 'Economic Crisis, Austerity and Trade Union Responses: The Irish Case in Comparative Perspective', *European Journal of Industrial Relations* 22, no. 2 (2016): 131–47.

7. There is no legal definition of precarious work, but it is universally understood to be a type of work which is poorly paid, unprotected and insecure. It is particularly prevalent in the private sector, especially service industries.

8. ICTU, *Shifting the Burden* (Dublin: ICTU, 2010), p. 10.

9. The agreement covered the different areas of the public sector and became known as the Croke Park Agreement because of the location of the talks.

10. Brian Sheehan, 'Employer Body Issues Bargaining Guidelines after Pulling out of National Pay Talks', Eurofound, 30 March 2010, www. eurofound.europa.eu/en/resources/article/2010/employer-body-issues-bargaining-guidelines-after-pulling-out-national-pay (last accessed 28 June 2024).

11. Trade union leaders who met with the Troika inspectors on their quarterly reviews found that, relative to the ECB and EU, the IMF representatives were more rational in their approach, recognising that cutting spending and increasing taxes was the opposite of what was needed to restore the Irish economy.

12. The WRC took over the functions of the Labour Relations Commission (LRC), the National Employment Rights Authority, the Equality Tribunal and the first-instance functions of the Employment Appeals Tribunal in 2015.

13. Eugene Hickland and Tony Dundon, 'The Shifting Contours of Collective Bargaining in the Manufacturing Sector in the Republic of Ireland: Government, Employer and Union Responses since the Economic Crisis', *European Journal of Industrial Relations* 22, no. 3 (2016), pp. 235–94.

14. Brian Sheehan, 'Public Sector Unions Agree to New Deal', Eurofound, 12 September 2013, www.eurofound.europa.eu/en/resources/article/2013/public-sector-unions-agree-new-deal (last accessed 28 June 2024).

15. This commitment had already been contained in the defeated Croke Park Two plan.

16. See Chapter 2 for more detail on this campaign.

17. See Chapter 3 for more about this.

18. For more on the housing movement see Chapter 5.

19. European Commission, 'Financial assistance to Ireland', https://economy-finance.ec.europa.eu/eu-financial-assistance/euro-area-countries/financial-assistance-ireland_en (last accessed 28 June 2024).

20. Vincenzo Maccarone and Roland Erne, 'Ireland: Trade Unions Recovering after Being Tipped off Balance by the Great Recession?', in Jeremy Waddington, Torsten Müller and Kurt Vandaele (eds.), *Trade Unions in the European Union: Picking up the Pieces from the Neoliberal Challenge* (Brussels: Peter Lang, 2023), pp. 585–624.

7

The Centre Left

Paul Dillon

The Irish Labour Party is today in a state of peril. No longer the half party in a two-and-a-half-party system, the party, according to opinion polls, is increasingly squeezed. Labour continues to stand over – indeed, promotes – its role in the 2011–16 government. But public support has flowed away; not only did it experience decline during its period in government, but polls also show the party is weaker now than when it exited government in 2016.

In previous decades, Labour lost support while in government and recovered thereafter. But the party has now broken this tradition, as its decline in support has continued in opposition.

This chapter assesses the performance of Labour in government from 2011 to 2016 and interrogates some of the claims of the party regarding its role. It concludes with some assessments regarding the party's present position and future prospects.

THE ROAD TO 2011

Before the crash, at the time of the 2007 election, there was a widespread assumption that the economic growth of the Celtic Tiger would last forever. Labour had allied with the centre-right Fine Gael in an electoral pact, the 'Mullingar Accord', which was endorsed by the party conference in 2005. Among the small number of dissenting voices to this pact were the Amalgamated Transport and General Workers' Union (ATGWU) trade union (later renamed Unite the Union), the youth section of the party, and the TD for Dublin North-East, Tommy Broughan. In his speech to delegates, Broughan quoted the ATGWU document which, referring to Fine

Gael, posed this rhetorical question: 'We can make them or break them. So why don't we break them?'

Fine Gael had dropped 23 seats in the 2002 election, and opponents of the Mullingar Accord argued the pact would revive Fine Gael fortunes rather than benefit Labour. They argued it would give Fine Gael credibility in the public eye by allowing them to pose as the only option for those wanting to replace the Fianna Fáil-led government. They were to be proven right. Fine Gael would win back nearly all the seats it had lost at the previous election in 2007, while Labour emerged with one less seat than they had going in.

The Mullingar Accord offered Fine Gael and Labour together as running mates to the electorate in 2007, although each party had a different manifesto. For its part, Labour was keen to reassure the electorate that any change in government would not lead to radical change. For example, on taxation, the party was keen to emphasise that 'taxes were down, and they're staying down'. At the party conference held in Dublin City University, the message was that Labour would not disrupt the dominant social and economic model of the time. However, this message was challenged by an intervention by future president Michael D. Higgins, who delivered a wide-ranging and blistering critique of the Celtic Tiger. In 2011, voters, still reeling from the aftermath of the economy's collapse, endorsed his vision and elected him president of Ireland. But that was the future.

Labour emerged from the 2007 election with only 20 seats, and, after waiting for a period of weeks, perhaps to test the political waters, Pat Rabbitte resigned as leader. He was replaced by Eamon Gilmore, who was elected uncontested. It wasn't long before the economic miracle, praised by Labour just months before, began to turn into a nightmare.

THE ROAD TO GOVERNMENT

In the period between 2007 and 2009, support for Labour grew. In particular, the bank guarantee was to be a major turning point in the party's fortune.

Irish banks had become massively exposed through property speculation, and, in October 2008, the government guaranteed all deposits and debts of the six main Irish banks and their subsidiaries abroad. The government gave the impression this was going to be the cheapest bank rescue in the world. In fact, Ireland would pay 42 per cent of the total cost of the European banking crisis, at a cost of close to €9,000 per person.[1]

While both Labour and Sinn Féin voted against the final measure to approve the bank guarantee on 17 October 2008,[2] an earlier vote to approve the guarantee in principle on 28 September had been backed by Sinn Féin and opposed by the Labour Party. The decision to vote against the bank guarantee was a principled one for Labour, but it came about after a degree of soul searching and internal debate. There was some considerable support for the proposal initially. Leading the charge to oppose the bank guarantee were Joan Burton, Michael D. Higgins and Tommy Broughan. Broughan would later be expelled from the Labour Party, in 2011, for voting against an extension of the bank guarantee when it was put forward by the then Fine Gael and Labour government.

Changes in the opinion polls were clear and somewhat predictable. Cuts introduced by the government in the 2009 budget were deeply unpopular and came on the back of the bank guarantee, which was viewed suspiciously by large sections of the public. It would become far more unpopular as time went on. It was clear that the lessons of the Mullingar Accord had been learned, at least in part. Labour ditched the idea of an electoral alliance with Fine Gael and the party started to be rewarded for presenting itself as an independent force to the public.

The other major event of this period was Ireland's entry into an Economic Adjustment Programme (EAP), commonly referred to as the 'bailout'. Just over two years on from the bank guarantee, in December 2010, Ireland applied for 'bailout' funds of €67.5 billion, overseen by the ECB, IMF, and European Commission (the 'Troika'). Ireland was to be part of this 'bailout' programme from December 2010 to December 2013. The programme was also funded by a further €17.5 billion of funds from the National Pension Reserve Fund. The entry into the bailout was to mark the beginning of the end of the government and was a crucial turning point for the Irish public debate.

From 2007 to 2011, Labour saw its support effectively double. At one stage, the party was ahead of Fine Gael in the polls and Eamon Gilmore came to be seen as an alternative Taoiseach. Perhaps Labour would break the mould of Irish politics and disrupt the pattern established by twentieth-century convention? Ultimately, this wasn't to happen, but the rise in support for the party contains some potentially interesting lessons.

In truth, the party leadership was nervous of presenting Labour to the electorate as a party which would lead a government. The initiative was taken by a group of Labour Youth members, led by the Chair of Labour Youth, who smuggled in 'Gilmore for Taoiseach' placards to the Labour conference in 2008 against the wishes of party officials. The leadership would later express the view that such placards should have gone through the party standing orders committee. Despite this opposition, the Gilmore for Taoiseach initiative would become a key element of the party approach during the period 2008–11. The party's independent status and the fact that it was seen potentially as an alternative government was rewarded at the polls.

The party was seen to stand alone, and a clear cleavage emerged between Labour and other parties. The party conference of 2008, in which Eamon Gilmore seemed to draw a line under the past and to present Labour as a clearly different option in Irish politics, marked another turning point. At that conference, Gilmore announced: 'The people who got us into this mess have no answer now.' It was as bold a political message as you would hear in mainstream Irish politics during that period.

Ultimately, in the runup to the general election in February 2011, the party was eclipsed by Fine Gael. Both Labour and Fine Gael had endorsed the National Recovery Plan 2011 to 2014, which was announced by the Fianna Fáil government in 2010 prior to the ballot, but which would become the blueprint economic policy for Ireland during the bailout period. As the election grew closer, Labour seemed to align more with Fine Gael and Fianna Fáil, blunting its own more distinct and independent approach, and support for the party gradually tailed off. For example, it made it clear to the electorate, through national media interviews, that there would be significant spending cuts. Differences with Fine

Gael focused on the speed of the adjustment that would take place, with Fine Gael pressing a case to front load spending cuts, while Labour suggested dragging them out over a longer period. There were also some differences regarding the ratio in spending cuts to tax increases proposed by the parties. The party leadership felt that media hostility to Labour leading a government played a significant role in the decline of support for the party.

In the years leading up to Labour entering government, it also made distinct moves to change how it operated internally. A commission on the future of the party, which reported to the party conference in 2009, proposed weakening the relationship between the party and the trade unions. This was defeated, with strong opposition led in part by Labour Youth and Mick O'Reilly from Unite. But the commission did succeed in removing some of the powers that had been held by party members and succeeded in significantly centralising authority and decision making in the party around the party leadership.

The efforts to reduce the connection with the trade union movement were in the context of wider changes in industrial relations. In 2008, employers organisations had withdrawn cooperation from the national wage agreement structure, bringing down Ireland's 'social partnership' industrial relations infrastructure. The collapse of social partnership ushered in a period that saw trade unions organise a number of large demonstrations and campaigns. Trade Union membership rose significantly in 2009–10, as workers responded to the threat of job losses in the private sector and public sector spending cuts. Labour, Sinn Féin and the smaller left parties all supported these union campaigns, and all experienced growth in this period.

ENTERING GOVERNMENT

Labour's election campaign in 2011 will be remembered for two things. Firstly, there was a pledge by Eamon Gilmore that it would be 'Frankfurt's way or Labour's way', which was seen as a promise to renegotiate the terms of the bailout. No such negotiation would take place. Secondly, as the party leadership feared that the election would yield a Fine Gael majority, an ad campaign was launched attacking Fine Gael. The campaign listed the cuts planned by Fine

Gael in the style of an ad for Tesco supermarket, turning the Tesco slogan 'Every little helps' into 'Every little hurts'. The intention was to warn what a Fine Gael one-party government would do, but the campaign came back to haunt Labour. The listed cuts came to be introduced by the Fine Gael–Labour government, leading to claims of broken election promises.

On election day in February 2011, the party emerged with 39 seats, which was the best result ever achieved by the party in its history. However, this outcome represented a significant decline from the party's highpoint in support when it received 33 per cent in a September 2010 poll. After the election, the two parties met and agreed a *Programme for Government*.

The Labour Party debated whether to endorse the *Programme for Government* at a meeting in Dublin on 6 March 2011. The *Programme for Government* was delivered, freshly printed, from the hands of party workers as delegates entered the hall. The ink on the document was still drying as delegates read it. The text was barely examined and barely discussed. Although SIPTU President Jack O'Connor, who clearly had managed to read it, delivered a warning of its contents, nevertheless, he argued for its acceptance saying, 'It was the best of the alternatives available.'[3] Unite opposed Labour's entry into government, and Unite would go on to disaffiliate from the Labour Party in 2012. Within a few years, there would be no trade unions affiliated to the Labour Party.

Only one TD spoke against the motion to endorse the *Programme for Government* and enter office: Tommy Broughan from Dublin North-East. There would have been more speeches against entry into government were it not for the fact that some delegates, who had been prominent members of the national executive, were refused entry into the hall. In the end, the party membership endorsed the motion to enter government by more than 90 per cent.

It is worth noting that there was no debate on alternative proposals about entering government with Fine Gael within the party membership or leadership. Despite the fact that a non-Fine Gael-led government was numerically possible, and that Labour had on paper the numbers to lead a government, the possibility was not entertained. Nor was the option of supporting a government under 'confidence and supply' ever considered.[4]

IN OFFICE 2011 TO 2016

Assessing Labour's role in government requires an understanding of how the party sees that period. At the outset, the party believed it had achieved some major gains. Fine Gael contested the election arguing the budget adjustment should be a 3:1 ratio of spending cuts to tax increases. Labour argued it should be a 1:1 split. The compromise was to be around 2:1. Fine Gael wanted the budget deficit to be under 3 per cent by 2014, Labour by 2016. The compromise was 2015.[5] The government would call a referendum on gay marriage, which was a proposal contained in the Labour manifesto and not the Fine Gael one. The party would make much of the government reversing a cut in the national minimum wage introduced by the previous coalition. This cut was emblematic of Ireland's response to the crisis. But although endorsed in the bailout programme document,[6] it was introduced prior to the bailout as part of the National Recovery Plan 2011 to 2014.[7] A trade-off conceded to Fine Gael for the restoration of the minimum wage was a tax cut for employers. In the end, the reversal of this cut only kept the minimum wage where it had been and the real value of the minimum wage, adjusted for prices, would fall between 2010 and 2011.

Other claims made by the party should be checked, particularly the facts concerning the terms of the bailout. One claim made repeatedly by back-bench TDs was that the state would run out of money unless the government had pursued the strategy it did. In reality, the state was fully funded for the duration of the 'bailout', as the Troika made clear.

Labour ministers would also claim that the state was no longer in control of its own chequebook.[8] For such a claim to stand up, it would have to be accepted that the government had no choice about what to spend and what to cut. The Troika made it clear that they were agnostic about how the ratios between spending cuts and tax increases were introduced; these were entirely a matter for the government.

Some Labour figures have claimed that were it not for their participation in government there would have been a fire sale of public assets. But, in the *Programme for Government*, Labour and

Fine Gael committed to a 'target up to 2 billion in sales of non-strategic state assets', leading to some significant privatisations. These included the National Lottery, the sale of Bord Gáis energy, sale of overseas power plants held by ESB and the privatisation of the state share in Aer Lingus. While these sales met with the approval of the Troika, there is little evidence that the Troika actually sought any further privatisations of state assets. Despite the eagerness of Fine Gael to privatise state assets, there is little evidence of any major disagreement between Labour and Fine Gael on this.

Perhaps the most significant claim of all made by Labour figures is that the actions taken by the coalition from 2011 to 2016 laid the basis for the increase in foreign direct investment which drove the recovery. Again, this claim has been disputed. In *The Politics of Capitalist Diversity in Europe: Explaining Ireland's Divergent Recovery from the Euro Crisis*, Samuel Brazys and Aidan Regan write, 'Ireland's economic recovery has little, if anything, to do with austerity induced cost competitiveness. Rather it is the outcome of an activist state-led enterprise policy aimed at "picking winners" from Silicon Valley.'[9]

There are some areas, however, where Labour's claims regarding their influence on government are more cut-and-dry. In relation to the equal right to marriage for gay and lesbian couples, Labour committed unequivocally to a referendum on equal marriage in its 2011 manifesto, unlike Fine Gael. Without Labour it seems unlikely that the referendum would have happened. But any electoral boost that the party may have expected from its association with the issue never happened. By the time the referendum was held, all of the major Irish parties supported it, leaving no space for a cleavage to emerge on the issue, as had happened in earlier decades around social issues like divorce and abortion. Research conducted by the party early in its period in government laid the basis for an apparent pivot towards liberal issues; the research, which emanated from focus groups, made an assumption that sustaining working-class votes would be a challenge, but that an electoral base could be further developed amongst middle and upper-middle strata voters, which would sustain the party. Only the first assumption would come to pass.

Labour retains some pride in measures introduced on workers' rights during the period. These measures were, in the main, introduced during the second half of the government when Ged Nash was a minister in the Department of Enterprise, and many were heavily influenced by trade unions such as SIPTU. The establishment of the Low Pay Commission, for example, was a significant development.

The attitudes of the EU institutions towards fiscal policy have changed significantly in the years since Labour and Fine Gael were in government together. While Labour can argue that the space for negotiation between 2011 and 2016 was unfavourable at EU level, the government did not participate in any significant efforts with other countries who were then part of a bailout programme to change the direction of EU policy. Indeed, the Minister for Finance in the government, Michael Noonan, went out of his way to disassociate Ireland from Greece.

It is clearly true that the government was restricted during 2011 to 2016. Not being able to borrow from markets, it was reliant on Troika funding. While some parts of the bailout package were implemented fully by the Fine Gael–Labour coalition, other parts were not.

The outsourcing of services for jobseekers was heavily favoured by the Troika, and it happened relatively early in the 2011 to 2016 government. Studies, including some by the Department of Social Protection itself, have shown the outsourcing of such services to have been ineffective. It was an example of a policy framework favoured by the Troika and implemented by the government that would not achieve its intended outcome. One Troika policy, supported by the government, which would achieve its aim, was returning the main banks in the state to profitability. When the bailout formally ended in 2013, the Troika left with a parting shot; a focus on bank profitability was to be key. A main way of doing this was to pursue essentially a reflation of the Irish housing market during 2011 to 2016. This policy of driving up house prices would, of course, have huge ramifications for many people living in Ireland.

But the government also failed to implement some aspects of the bailout programme. Plans to introduce water charges were ultimately not introduced following a campaign of public protest. Similarly, a commitment to liberalise the law profession and introduce competition, which the Troika were keen on, never really came to pass. Minister for Justice Alan Shatter's Legal Services Regulation Act 2015 did not lead to the sort of competition in the legal services areas which the Troika envisaged. Shatter would attribute Labour opposition at cabinet as one of the impediments to serious reform.

In the local election of 2014, Labour got only 7.2 per cent of the vote. Dissatisfaction with the outcome led to an internal party revolt and the resignation of party leader Eamon Gilmore. He was replaced by Joan Burton. Dissatisfaction with election results or opinion polls would later end the leaderships of Joan Burton, Brendan Howlin and Alan Kelly, before Ivana Bacik took over party leadership in 2022. Between 2011 and 2016, the party would remove the whip from five TDs (another, Willie Penrose, lost his place in government but not the role of party whip). One of these TDs, Roisin Shortall, would go on to co-found a new political party, the Social Democrats, in 2015. This party fought the general election of 2016 partly on the basis of opposition to tax cuts. Such a clear policy benefited the Social Democrats, who returned three TDs at that election and have grown since. Labour fought in the same campaign in 2016 mainly on its record in government and signalled an intention to participate in a continuation of the Fine Gael-led coalition. In the event, Labour returned seven TDs and achieved 6.6 per cent of the vote. (Its support has since dropped even further.) After the election, there were indications that the party leadership and parliamentary group wanted to join a Fine Gael coalition, a position favoured by many party big hitters, including former MEP Proinsias De Rossa. After some rebellion in the ranks of party members, represented in groups like the party executive and the General Council, the party headed for the opposition benches, where it has remained ever since.

PRESENT AND FUTURE

The Labour Party has made no effort to distance itself from the 2011 to 2016 government. It stands over its time in office. There has been no Fianna Fáil-type apology, like that offered by its leader Micheál Martin to distance himself from the government he had participated in from 2007 to 2011. Labour figures generally view their time in government in a favourable light; the general public view of Labour participation in government is somewhat less favourable. The party has a particular problem with younger voters; just 2 per cent of voters under 35 backed the party in a recent poll. The party's difficulties chime with a challenging moment for social democratic parties across Europe.

Party figures can certainly lay claim to a distinct tradition in Irish politics. The question going forward will be whether or not the party can ever effectively recover from the legacy of the 2011 to 2016 period. Some party spokespeople, for example Senator Marie Sherlock, have demonstrated how the party can be distinctive in areas such as workers' rights. However, Labour is still struggling to find its voice in a crowded, competitive political field in Ireland.

Perhaps ironically, support in Ireland for leftwing policies is now far greater than ever before, in particular amongst younger people. The cause for this surge in support can primarily be identified as the consequences of the financial crisis. Labour, in government when the crisis bit most ferociously and standing over that government's policies, has not been able to ride the wave of interest in leftwing policies.

NOTES

1. Ann Cahill, '42% of Europe's Banking Crisis Paid by Ireland', *Irish Examiner*, 16 January 2013, www.irishexaminer.com/news/arid-20219 703.html (last accessed 28 June 2024).
2. 'Dail Approves Bank Guarantee Scheme', *Irish Independent*, 17 October 2008, www.independent.ie/business/dail-approves-bank-guarantee-scheme/26485414.html (last accessed 28 June 2024).
3. Áine Kerr, 'Smiles All Round as 90pc of Labour Party Backs Deal', *Irish Independent*, 7 March 2011, www.independent.ie/irish-news/smiles-all-round-as-90pc-of-labour-party-backs-deal/26711131.html (last accessed 28 June 2024).
4. Under 'confidence and supply', Labour would not be part of the government but would vote with the government. This approach was used by Fianna Fáil when they supported the 2016–20 government.

5. Eamon Gilmore, *Inside the Room: The Untold Story of Ireland's Crisis Government* (Newbridge: Merrion Press, 2015), p. 83.

6. European Commission, *The Economic Adjustment Programme for Ireland*, February 2011, https://ec.europa.eu/economy_finance/publications/occasional_paper/2011/pdf/ocp76_en.pdf (last accessed 28 June 2024).

7. Government of Ireland, *The National Recovery Plan 2011–2014*, November 2010, https://enterprise.gov.ie/en/publications/publication-files/for f%C3%A1s/the-national-recovery-plan-2011-2014.pdf (last accessed 28 June 2024).

8. Marie O'Halloran and Michael O'Regan, 'Quinn "Examining" Education Funding Report', *The Irish Times*, 16 November 2011, www.irishtimes.com/news/quinn-examining-education-funding-report-1.887153 (last accessed 28 June 2024).

9. Samuel Brazys and Aidan Regan, 'The Politics of Capitalist Diversity in Europe: Explaining Ireland's Divergent Recovery from the Euro Crisis', *Perspectives on Politics* 15, no. 2 (2017): 411–27, https://doi.org/10.1017/S1537592717000093.

8

Anarchism

Kevin Doyle

In 2009, the Workers Solidarity Movement (WSM) was 25 years old. Although not the only anarchist organisation on the island of Ireland, it was easily the most active and visible. Numerically, it had around 50 active members,[1] with several branches in Dublin, a vibrant branch in Cork, and a branch in Belfast. It has also had a network of supporters and contacts around the country, with reasonable prospects of establishing stable branches in other towns and cities.[2]

On Ireland's left, the WSM had established its presence. It frequently took a leading role in social struggles. Its longevity stood to it, as did its reputation for honest activism and an unsectarian approach. Ten thousand copies of its newspaper, *Workers Solidarity*, came out every two months and were distributed door-to-door.[3] Occasionally, this was even increased to 15,000 or 20,000 copies for special issues.[4] And it had a sizeable presence online. If any political organisation was capable of capitalising on what was ahead, it could be argued it should have been the WSM.

However, in 2009, significant divisions existed, and over the next number of years these would lead to a major fracturing inside the organisation; towards the end of the pandemic the organisation would be formally wound up. From the outside, the extent of the collapse that happened was surprising. Few would have predicted it or expected the demise to be so total. The organisation on many levels looked healthy. Equally, from inside the organisation, the degree of collapse took many by surprise. Splits in organisations are not uncommon, and indeed on the Irish left it is often joked that they are a formality to be endured – part of growing up. So why did the WSM sunder so fully in the way it did?

In this chapter I will address the trajectory of the WSM as it faced the economic crash and the subsequent fight against austerity. A neat story suggests itself: whereas the libertarian socialist movement fell away during the battle against austerity, the electoral left rode out struggle and has made considerable inroads on power. But this hardly seems an accurate account of what really happened on the ground. To use the example of Cork: the fight against austerity there was conducted by a broad alliance of activists – anarchists and aligned and non-aligned socialists. However, the fact that the Socialist Party eventually gained a Dáil seat in Cork (arising out of the general anti-austerity struggle there) is not confirmation that the Socialist Party was a dominant force – it wasn't. It was simply the organisation best placed to gain electorally from the community-based struggles that happened.

The reality that should really concern us, against which this account is offered, is the steady decline in working-class self-activity since around the mid-1980s. Trade unions are much weaker now than they were, and independent working-class self-organisation (in 'old-school speak', rank and file networks) is practically extinct. Indeed, it could be argued that, close to 15 years on from the crash, the Irish bourgeoisie has never had it so good. Even Irish rugby – a favourite plaything of theirs – is conquering all before it!

Returning to the WSM, I offer an interpretation of what happened. Because the WSM went into decline early in the 2010s, this chapter does not extend into the latter half of the decade. And because I argue that the decline in the early 2010s must be seen in relation to the previous development of the WSM, significant attention is paid to the rise of the WSM in the years leading up to 2008.

What happened was hardly straightforward or easily explained. Choices were made: some good, many bad. My perspective on the WSM, moreover, is also coloured by my being mainly involved with the WSM in Cork, whereas, in fact, some of the sharpest debates (and divisions) inside the movement occurred in Dublin.

Finally, many will not agree with me in terms of what I have focused on here, or with the weight I give to certain aspects of what happened. Other contributions have already been made by the different factions that formed inside the WSM as it fractured. There are truths as well as important observations made in all of these different examinations – even by those who rejected anarchism in the aftermath of the WSM splitting in Dublin.[5]

Anarchist activists must always be ready to learn. If we are hopeful that capitalism will be overturned one day – and personally I remain so – then we must live with these present difficulties, try to understand the mistakes that we made, and rebuild. It is the only way.

A BRIEF HISTORY

While anarchist organising on the island of Ireland goes back as far as the 1880s, its modern history really begins in the 1960s when a number of anarchist groups and initiatives started. Over the 1960s, 1970s and 1980s, various anarchist groups, publications and bookshops were founded and disappeared. However, in late 1983, anarchist and anarchist groups around Ireland were invited to a conference called to begin the work of building a 'coherent national anarchist organisation'.[6] Sixteen activists attended the Saturday meeting with over half returning the following day. The conference gave itself six months in which to develop further these core points of common ground, and this led directly to the founding conference of the WSM in Cork on the 15/16 September 1984.[7] A new monthly anarchist newspaper, *Workers Solidarity*, was proposed, with an initial print run of 1,000. It would sell for 20p and would have a dual role: to print news on current struggles and to advance and explain what anarchism stood for.

The decision to form a new 'class struggle'-oriented anarchist organisation was a significant step forward, with many of those involved optimistic about the prospects. They believed that if anarchists developed and practised a more organised form of their ideas, they'd win support. A longstanding millstone around the neck of the anarchist tradition has been its association with disorganisation and scattergun activism. If this bogeyman could be dealt with, anarchist ideas and practice could gain traction. Without doubt, and perhaps in the main due to its early overconfidence, the WSM in 1984 grossly underestimated the scale of the task ahead.

TO SURVIVE IS EVERYTHING

What would also turn out to be of considerable significance was the precarious state of the class struggle. Those involved in the WSM were activists with varying degrees of involvement in trade unionism. Also difficult to gauge was the lie of the land ahead. In essence – although this wasn't visible at the time – the WSM was founded at the tail-end of an important period of independent working-class activity. The Irish working class in the 1970s had a name for being strike-happy. While the nature of struggles had turned decidedly defensive in the early 1980s as the recession hit, the level of union activism and militancy was still quite high.

The recession that developed in Ireland through the 1980s dampened all this down, but there was worse to come. Large-scale capitalist restructuring was getting underway, and the beginning of globalised production methods witnessed employers flexing their muscles using a powerful new tactic: *take what we offer or we'll move to another country.* When this happened in a number of disputes, the overall impact was chilling. The balance of forces began to shift decidedly in the mid-1980s as the WSM took to the streets. The degree to which it would shift was something that few would anticipate.

Nonetheless, *Workers Solidarity* was a success. It was sold outside many workplaces in Cork and Dublin, outside dole offices, at protests, in colleges and in pubs. Appearing regularly and on time, its general newsiness made it popular.

During these early years of its existence, the WSM engaged with a range of struggles and disputes, reporting on them and offering analysis, and worked in a variety of solidarity groups around strikes and disputes. Despite the apparent outward success, internally the organisation was already under pressure and stretched.

Following a series of disputes, both the Dublin and Cork branches lost members. *Workers Solidarity* didn't appear for over a year, and during that time the organisation fought to stay afloat and reposition itself. The expectation remained that anarchists should be involved at their workplaces and in helping with any ongoing political campaigns, but now there was a greater appreciation that not burning out the remaining activists was also vital to survival. Fortunately, the organisation stayed afloat and, independently, a layer of students with ideas close to those of the WSM made contact and later joined the organisation.

Generally though, the political climate was poor, particularly in the workplace. Under the duress of the 1980s recession, a process of social partnership (between workers and employers) was promoted and took hold. Employers and the trade union bureaucracy entered into a peaceful co-existence that was sold to the membership on the basis that 'a little' (in terms of wage rises) is better than being on the dole. WSM members would take part in a series of campaigns to oppose these agreements, but each one was lost. Strike action declined precipitously as Ireland was increasingly marketed as a positive and welcoming location for multinationals looking to make money by avoiding paying tax. In an important and detrimental way, workplace struggle changed for the worse. To talk about and recall 'shop-steward committees' was almost like talking about a period before the last ice age.

Outside Ireland, something else significant took place. The emergence of the Zapatista movement was an important beacon of hope at this time. Here was a movement that was courageous, anti-capitalist and autonomous.

Closer to home a further, significant campaign was building up steam. As part of the new neoliberal agenda, local councils were putting many of their services out for privatisation. One such service was the collection of domestic rubbish, where the first step in privatisation was the introduction of a waste collection charge known as the 'bin tax'. The anti-bin tax campaign would rumble on over many years and would ultimately be defeated, but it was important in the role it had in bringing the WSM into the middle of community-based struggle that was of course strongest in working-class communities. Also, for the first time in a substantive way, anarchists were pitted against the electoral left in a clear way, and to a point where they were able to win the arguments. But the anti-bin tax campaign would also highlight a dangerous weakness in the anarchist approach. They could be the best activists and the most energetic foot-soldiers, but it was the political organisations that argued for participation in the electoral process – the Socialist Party and Sinn Féin – who would benefit in the sense of gaining seats at the table of power. That said, participation in the anti-bin tax campaign was largely positive for the WSM to the extent that it helped the organisation regain confidence in the project it was involved in.

THE FORK IN THE ROAD

The new millennium ushered in a crucial decade for the WSM. It had survived a series of setbacks. Despite its small core size, it continued to produce a range of written material pushing its anarchist analysis: a newspaper, a magazine and leaflets specific to particular issues. It was present at almost all major political events, and also ran regular branch meetings and open-to-the-public discussions on the issues of the day. Additionally, it was active internationally in the anarchist movement, building links with other like-minded tendencies.

All of this demanded a consistently high level of commitment, work and activism from its members. While some found this aspect of the WSM attractive – an indication of seriousness – others voiced doubts; supporters of the WSM who were asked to become members often replied that they didn't feel they would be able for the level of work required of being a member. Visitors from outside Ireland, interested in the WSM and the type of organisation it was, were often taken aback to learn how small the organisation actually was. To some, it was amazing that it was able to do so much.

To a point, its work rate was a reflection of its tight political basis. But its productivity was also undoubtedly a product of the calibre of activists it had managed to attract, many of whom gave unselfishly to the cause. Not unreasonably, though, the focus was turning to growth. Growth would alleviate some of the workload issues, but it also made plain common sense in terms of ever getting places: to have more impact the WSM needed to be bigger.

At this point the organisation began lowering the level of political agreement needed for membership. As it did so, an important division of views emerged in the organisation. One argued that the conditions for a large anarchist movement to exist in Ireland simply weren't there. Revolutionary organisations could only become large in revolutionary times and Ireland at the turn of the millennium was far from that. Far better, this view argued, to remain politically unified and coherent, even if smaller; after all, it was this strategy that had got the WSM to where it was.

The argument that WSM shouldn't open its doors fully and seek to become as large as possible seemed counterintuitive to others. This view argued that the WSM was only just starting to make its mark. Lots of people liked the organisation and its unsectarian approach. It was very active, libertarian and solidly reliable. Some of the things the WSM had hoped to bring to the anarchist hymn sheet were now in fact beginning to pay off: this was the WSM's practical and organised portrayal of anarchist politics. Why not cash in and get as many to join as possible?

However, the knot the WSM found itself in was more than just about these choices. The level of activity and input for its small membership was quite high. Was this sustainable and for how long? Even at this point the WSM had failed to identify any clear milestones that it needed to reach. Numerical size was about the only metric that anyone could agree on. It was already evident that some were joining the WSM not because of its anarchist views but because it was simply the most active and militant group in Ireland.

Also critical at this point was the organisation's engagement with the class struggle. While a number of members practised what they preached and were active inside established unions, many others were in precarious work situations or were students; others were not involved at all.

Two other events would now further catalyse the WSM's orientation to becoming a more open, larger and more populist organisation. The first was the emergence of the anti-globalisation protests around Seattle that shook the consensus that neoliberalism was the new norm. The Battle of Seattle kicked off a series of mass mobilisations around the world which further energised an emerging and broad-based anti-capitalist movement.

In Ireland, the WSM played a role in organising a series of libertarian anti-capitalist conferences called the 'Grassroots Gatherings'. These took place in different parts of Ireland and, while difficult to pin down with any one description, drew significant numbers. Different campaigns – local, national and even international – took part. The strong participatory, non-hierarchical and communal nature of these gatherings made them popular, offering activists a positive social space to be in. Abortion rights, environmental action, resource exploitation and food politics were issues addressed.

The other political event of significance was the second US invasion of Iraq. The Irish left mobilised strongly around opposition to the war, but anarchists were to the fore in efforts to focus attention on the USA's plan to use Shannon Airport in Co. Clare as part of its supply line for the war. A specific anti-war initiative arose from one Grassroots Gathering, known as Grassroots Network Against War (GNAW). Committed to direct action around 'Shannon Warport', it quickly upset and outflanked the 'Let's not break the law' brigade then dominant on Ireland's left.

Recognising a possible danger, the Irish state mobilised. GNAW made headlines and, to an extent, this was useful for the anti-authoritarian left – long used to being ignored – but the reality was that these militant protests were easily contained by the state.

GNAW highlighted the political space that was there for taking on the state and disrupting 'business as usual'. Confronting the state was also energising for some. It drew lots of attention and drew some activists into the orbit of radical politics, but it was also gradually shifting the WSM as an organisation towards a 'substitutionist' mentality. If the general public wasn't prepared to fight, then the WSM would try to stoke it into action as best it could. Again, this fed the drive to be even bigger, to make the fight a little bit more even. But a question that really needed asking (and answering) is the one all socialists have had to face: can you really ever beat the state in a physical fight? There is only one way, and it's through building in the workplace, not on the streets.

Towards the end of the decade a serious cleavage had opened up. A central tenet of the WSM had been the idea that the organisation should agree a strategy and work for that collectively. But this was increasingly difficult to implement. One view that could be taken is that strategy was now being decided 'on the hoof', and to a point it was. A more pessimistic view was that the organisation had already irreversibly opted to go down the road of aligning itself towards an alternative anti-authoritarian constituency. As long as this constituency existed then it seemed that the WSM was doing the right thing. But the anti-capitalist movement was already in decline.

The significant tensions that existed inside the organisation, which to emphasise again were not helped by the heavy demands that the organisation continued to place on its members, came to the fore primarily, it should be said, in Dublin. A number of important things had also changed. The WSM has grown four-fold in a little over ten years. Numerically, it was now quite a different entity, yet the organisation had hardly addressed the changed dynamic in terms of functionality and cohesion. This was particularly evident at WSM conferences, the one occasion when all members could meet and be together. Formality and procedures took precedence over any team building or debate. The organisation was in a difficult period and yet it did not sit down to look at where it was, what resources it had at its disposal and, crucially, how it saw matters evolving.

Three key tensions were present: the organisation's relationship to the class struggle; the issue of purity versus populism; and the underrated matter of stamina and long-term survival. Those who favoured a much easier basis for membership reckoned that the WSM needed to push on and become even bigger. It needed to be an organisation of several hundred members instead of being content with being around 60 or so, as it was then. Also, if it was larger and more geographically spread, it couldn't be easily ignored. This might then catalyse the organisation to grow into an even larger size.

Some of the key assumptions underpinning this viewpoint rested heavily on the WSM itself and its agency: that the WSM could act independent of the political conditions around it. In other words, the actual state of the class struggle had almost become irrelevant to this view. At one point one of its proponents suggested that the WSM should aim to have 80 branches in a number of years. The disconnection from reality was stark.

BUST

When the economic crisis unfolded from late 2008 onwards, hard political reality returned to mainstream Irish life with a roar. Anger erupted at the scale of the debt crisis and the degree of financial mismanagement. For a brief moment Irish capitalism looked wounded, but with the aid of the European Union, the European Central Bank and the IMF, the situation was retrieved, and the tables ably turned on Ireland's working class. The old adage 'Never waste a good crisis' was used with deadly effect. Here and there, there was resistance, for example, with the pensioners over Medical Cards,[8] but there was also generalised dismay and resignation. As is nearly always the case with Ireland, emigration took off.

At the time, I wrote:

> The anarchist movement has not ... remained immune ... The lack of any serious fight back has seriously undermined morale. Moreover, the scale of this and the profound implications of what it indicates have exposed serious weaknesses in our own analysis and practice. While this is sobering and could be turned to some advantage, there is a developing sense also that there is no longer a clear understanding about how to move forward.[9]

In due course the crash would produce an opportunity for Ireland's left – particularly for those who were there and ready to grasp it, but it was primarily and in the first instance a crisis for many ordinary people. A significant section of Irish society grumbled but then accepted austerity. This came as a bitter blow to many who had been in the WSM for years.

Importantly, the WSM had little or no purchase in the area where signs of a fightback were taking root – working-class communities. In fact, it became clear at this point how mistaken the WSM's approach had been in the period before the crash. From the turn of the millennium, the WSM had rebuilt itself as an organisation. It had considerable energy and belief aplenty in its own self, but it had misspent this currency wantonly, directing a great deal of its energy towards the anti-capitalist movement.

Early in the crisis, WSM members threw themselves into supporting struggles against cuts and layoffs. When this early wave of struggles subsided, the WSM began behaving as though its anti-capitalist activism could act as a substitute for the self-activity of the working class. In 2008–9, WSM members supported the various mobilisations and workplace occupations that took place, and they put huge efforts into mobilising around the public sector strike on 24 November 2009, believing this could be the first step towards a general strike. However, when this failed to happen and social struggles began to subside, the WSM kept ploughing on at full speed despite being increasingly disconnected from wider struggles. A series of initiatives were pursued: Social Solidarity Network in late 2009, the anti-capitalist bloc in the Summer of 2010, and the 1% Network in late 2010 to early 2011. But none had any real base in or traction with the wider working class.

Ultimately, when it mattered, and where it mattered, the WSM had little to draw on in terms of doing anything meaningful about the huge pain being inflicted right across Irish society, and particularly on working-class communities. Little wonder it began to haemorrhage members. This process was not helped by the arrival of Occupy and the attempt by some in the WSM to endow this new iteration of anti-capitalism with great new powers.

In fact, resistance to austerity would gather around the Campaign Against the Household and Water Taxes. In both Cork and Dublin, members and former members of the WSM took part in this. In Cork, where the WSM also began losing members, the branch remained largely intact, particularly around the Solidarity Books initiative, which had served for a time as an organising centre for the anti-austerity campaign there. Cork WSM members played a significant part in building the anti-property tax campaign in the city, which later folded into the anti-water tax campaign. Indeed, many WSM and ex-WSM members continued their involvement in this movement until victory was achieved and the water tax abandoned by the government. However, organisationally, the WSM was now sinking, leaving the electoralist left capably positioned to capitalise on the large grassroots movement that had developed to fight the water tax.

In 2021, the WSM was formally wound up as an organisation.[10] From about 2015 onwards it was essentially one small branch in Dublin. The focus was on building 'new media' outlets, on exploiting the vast 'connectivity' potential of the internet, and on linking up with an intersectional approach to politics. This all largely came to nothing. Those remaining in the WSM ran out of energy and ideas, or both.

The winding up of the organisation places a full stop on the particular initiative that was the WSM. It is right then, that at this point, the difficult questions are asked. Is the task of building a viable political organisation in Ireland beyond anarchists? One aspect the WSM clearly underestimated was the dominance of electoralist-style politics in Ireland. This, together with the concurrent weakness in the class struggle, made progress challenging.

Were those who argued that the WSM should have stayed small and not overhyped its prospects and abilities perhaps correct all along? Or was the WSM wrongly calibrated from its first days? Indeed, in its early days the WSM set off like it was running a sprint but within a few years it became apparent that it was a marathon (if not a series of marathons) that it needed to be training for.

The Spanish anarchists argue that it takes three generations for a movement to be made. This also suggests the expectations of the WSM activists were wildly over optimistic. When issues to do with burnout and personality conflicts come to the fore, it is often indicative of wider political division. The WSM didn't properly consider the longer-term attrition of the project it was immersed in at all, perhaps because it didn't understand in the first place how big a project it had undertaken. Perhaps this was more than anything a reflection of the inexperience of its core membership.

It has been said to me that even though the WSM didn't come away with the scalp of capitalism, it made its mark, played a big part in many struggles, campaigns and fights, and helped in that way to make Ireland a better place to live. This is surely true, and it would be a mistake for any of us to underestimate the work done by anarchists in this respect.

Tellingly, at this point, it is in the workplace that capitalism has triumphed most – outflanking worker organisations through globalisation and atomising resistance where it can. Considering that elsewhere anarchists are often successful organisers in the arena of the class struggle, this core matter requires addressing by Ireland's anarchists as they regroup and rebuild for the next heave.

A new world in our hearts always.

NOTES

1. The number of members was far higher than the number of active members. James O'Brien estimates that it was over 80 (see note 5). As discussed later, the level of activity expected of 'active members' was very high.
2. WSM, 'The WSM is 25', *Workers Solidarity* 111, September 2009, www.wsm.ie/c/anarchism-action-wsm-25 (last accessed 28 June 2024).
3. *Ibid.*
4. This was done for special issues produced at the time of the first and second Lisbon Treaty referendums. See: WSM, 'WSM Activity in the Autumn of 2009', *Workers Solidarity* 112, November/December 2009, www.wsm.ie/c/wsm-activity-autumn-2009 (last accessed 28 June 2024); and WSM, 'Report on the Fall 2008 National Conference of the WSM', 9 November 2008, www.wsm.ie/c/report-autumn-2008-national-conference-wsm (last accessed 28 June 2024).
5. See: James O'Brien, 'The WSM and Anarchism: A Political Analysis', Spirit of Contradiction, 16 August 2012, https://spiritofcontradiction.eu/bronterre/2012/08/16/the-wsm-a-political-analysis (last accessed 28 June 2024); Andrew Flood, 'The WSM and Fighting the Last War – A Reply to James O'Brien', Anarchist Writers, 20 February 2013, https://anarchism.pageabode.com/the-wsm-fighting-the-last-war-a-reply-to-james-obrien/ (last accessed 28 June 2024); and Kevin Doyle, 'Anarchism, Ireland and the WSM', Kevin Doyle Blog, 2 June 2013, https://kfdoyle.wordpress.com/2013/06/02/anarchism-ireland-wsm/ (last accessed 28 June 2024).
6. Kevin Doyle personal archive.
7. *Ibid.*
8. Under the Irish welfare system, a medical card provides access to certain health services free of charge for those with income below an age-related threshold.
9. Doyle, 'Anarchism, Ireland and the WSM'.
10. WSM, 'Workers Solidarity Movement Closing Statement', 6 March 2023, www.wsm.ie/c/workers-solidarity-movement-closing-statement (last accessed 28 June 2024).

9

Trotskyism

David Landy

Few would have predicted the rollercoaster successes of Trotskyism in Ireland over the past 15 years. In common with other western countries, there had been countless different varieties of Trotskyism in the 1970s and 1980s, but by 2008 there were really only two parties left standing – the Socialist Party (SP) and the Socialist Workers Party (SWP). The SP, originally called Militant Tendency, had grown out of the left of the Labour Party, and, as with the English version, with which it was aligned, it was expelled from Labour in the 1980s. It renamed itself the Socialist Party in 1996 and maintained some presence in unions and in working-class Dublin areas where it had been prominent in opposing water charges in the 1990s and bin charges in the early 2000s. The SWP – again, aligned with the British organisation of the same name – was more based in university campuses, recruiting heavily from students, though they, too, began running candidates in elections in the 1990s, albeit with no success.

During the recession, their fortunes changed. Both the SP and the SWP were key components of every anti-austerity campaign throughout the decade. They contributed hugely to all the major and many of the minor campaigns of the era and were rewarded for their activities with electoral success and unprecedented media prominence. By 2020, both parties had collapsed – but while the SP collapsed in the customary way of Trotskyist parties, breaking up in a vicious internecine split, the SWP had, uniquely for a western Trotskyist party, collapsed into success, and had been swallowed up by its larger electoral vehicle, People Before Profit.

One question this chapter examines is why their fortunes diverged – why was the growth of the SWP sustained, whereas the SP stalled, even before its split? One possible answer is their approach towards campaigns. The SP favoured a more ideological, or, as they understood it, principled stance, generally taking a critical position towards other groups in the campaigns. This isolated it from those they worked with and created tensions not only between the SP and others but also within the organisation itself. The SWP were more flexible and willing to work with others, albeit on their own terms. Another explanation is that while the SP was, however unwillingly, dragged into the centre of splits in the British organisation, the SWP adroitly managed to avoid involvement in the scandals engulfing their British namesake.

However, the story of Trotskyism in this period is more than splits, it is how both groups played a sustained and central part in anti-austerity campaigning, and in the process placed Trotskyism – again, uniquely in western countries – at the heart of leftwing opposition to austerity, as well as in the national and local legislatures.

ELECTORAL FORTUNES AND ELECTORAL FRONTS

One measure of how the parties fared is their electoral results. For ten years, 1997–2007, the SP representative for Dublin West, Joe Higgins, was the only Trotskyist in the Dáil, treated as a harmless oddity and occasional nuisance. He lost his seat in the 2007 election, a sign of the weakness of Trotskyism in Ireland before the recession. Equally, his election to the European Parliament in 2009 was a harbinger of changed fortunes. In 2011, in the election in which the Labour Party won 37 seats, the SP won two Dáil seats, as did People Before Profit (PBP). All the seats were in Dublin, and included Joe Higgins winning back his Dublin West seat. His European seat was rotated to his party colleague, the then unknown Paul Murphy.

Murphy lost the seat in the 2014 European elections, partly because PBP ran a candidate against him, Bríd Smith, splitting the left vote. Nevertheless, both parties did well in the local elections on the same day. They built on this success in the 2016 elections, contesting them together under the cumbersome name Anti-Austerity Alliance – People Before Profit and winning six seats, three a piece – including their first seat outside Dublin, with Mick Barry of the SP elected in the working-class constituency of Cork North Central. Their vote share also went up from 2.2 per cent to 3.9 per cent between the two elections.

Table 9.1   Local election seats

	SP/AAA/Solidarity seats	SP/AAA/Solidarity votes	SWP/PBP seats	SWP/PBP votes
2005	4 (SP)	13,494	0 (SWP)	6,125
2009	4 (SP)	16,052	5 (PBP)	15,879
2014	14 (AAA)	21,097	14 (PBP)	29,051
2019	4 (Solidarity)	10,911	7 (PBP)	21,972
2024	3 (Solidarity)	4,952	10 (PBP)	22,231

As Table 9.1 shows, their votes in local elections showed a steady rise during the recession, though it also demonstrates the growing popularity of the SWP/PBP as opposed to the previously dominant SP. Before the recession, the SP had more reach than the SWP, with a small but real community-based organisation. This reversed over the decade, and when both their votes shrank in 2019, it did so more calamitously for the SP than the SWP/PBP. In 2024, the decline of the vote for the SP continued, while it stabilised for PBP.

In the 2020 general election, even though their combined vote went down to 2.6 per cent, they escaped with only losing one TD. This was largely because Sinn Féin ran too few candidates, which meant that a lot of their surplus votes were transferred left, to Trotskyist candidates. But parity in strength between the two groups wasn't maintained. PBP managed to keep its three TDs, while Solidarity kept only one, with Paul Murphy running separately under the RISE (Revolutionary, Internationalist, Socialist and Environmentalist) moniker, which he was later to amalgamate within PBP.

As can be seen, one feature of both parties was the frequent name changes of their electoral vehicles, which often confused even close observers. These name changes weren't whimsical or unimportant features. They represented one of the chief aims of both parties in this period, which was to reach outside their tightly knit cadre of party members and found or join a broad organisation that would harness working-class anger and mobilise a wider constituency towards change. It's fair to say that the SP utterly failed to create that vehicle, while the SWP achieved modest success in this regard.

The SWP had formed PBP in 2005 and, after drawing in some non-SWP activists, contested the 2009 local elections under this brand.[1] But in reality, PBP didn't have much more than a paper existence until about 2013, not even holding a proper conference in this eight-year period. In 2014, the SP also formed an electoral front group, the Anti-Austerity Alliance (AAA), which they renamed Solidarity in 2017. Like the SWP's front group, while AAA/Solidarity included some non-SP members, it was controlled by the party.

TYING CATS IN A BAG – THE UNITED LEFT ALLIANCE

The (re)launch of PBP and AAA came after the failure of a significant attempt to form a broad leftwing party. This was the United Left Alliance (ULA), which initially came together as an electoral alliance for the 2011 elections. Following these elections, there were serious attempts to turn it into a broad left party. Especially important in this were the unusually large number of non-SP and non-SWP members in the ULA, comprising about a third of the membership. The failure of the ULA was subsequently blamed on both the SP and SWP, with critics citing personality clashes and obscurantist factionalism that prevented the two Trotskyist groups from uniting. But in truth, the differences between the two parties were real and substantial, in terms of both policy and orientation.

At the start of the recession, the SP would have considered themselves more embedded in communities and with more focus on working-class concerns, rather than frenetically jumping from fashionable campaign to campaign, which the SWP was accused of. The SP also argued that as they took their socialism seriously, they were less susceptible to the siren song of nationalism than the SWP. As a result, the SP were very critical of Sinn Féin's nationalism, and sought to include the Protestant working class in Northern Ireland in their work. The SWP, in turn, spoke of the importance of being involved in New Social Movements as a way of drawing in younger people, and as an indication that they were more open to intersectional analyses of capitalism and offered a greater place to issues of gender and race, rather than simply a monotone focus on class. They were also more sympathetic to republicanism, arguing that this was due to a robust critique of imperialism and colonialism – whether in Northern Ireland or Palestine – which the SP had failed to develop.

These differences weren't trivial and are why both parties remained wary of calls to a unity that simply involved an amalgamation of their organisations, seeing no value in unity unless it could help build an expanding movement of the working class. Nevertheless, there was a huge commonality of ideas and approaches between the parties, and members found themselves on the same side of the barricades time and again. Equally, in local election in 2014, both parties tried to stay out of each other's way, generally not contesting constituencies where the other was strongest in order not to spoil each other's chances.[2]

The ill-tempered but substantive debates over the ULA were important in presenting the differences between the parties on the role of socialist praxis in building a united left.[3] The fundamental difference was over the question of purism or, alternatively, of principle. The SP criticised the SWP for trying to bury socialism in its election literature, accusing the SWP of doing little more than calling for cosmetic changes in capitalism, for fear of scaring off possible voters. The SWP denied the allegation that they were reformist rather than revolutionary, claiming they were working towards a socialist transformation of society as much as the SP. But in order to build a broad left alternative they needed to avoid tired socialist jargon that was incomprehensible to the working class as it actually was. Linked to this were differing attitudes to the Labour Party. The SP advocated a total exclusion of austerity-introducing Labour politicians from any platform. The SWP wanted a more open policy towards them and others on the soft left as a way of broadening the movement. There were similar differences on their position towards Sinn Féin. As might be expected, the SP took a more hardline approach, seeing them as a nationalist formation, comfortable with neoliberalism, while the SWP was far more open to working within them. There were also other significant issues, such as organising in the North (SP was against the ULA having a presence in the North, SWP in favour), between the parties.

Despite these policy differences, there were attempts by both the SP and the SWP to develop the ULA into a united party in 2011. What sank it was more than policy differences or even understandable distrust between the two parties. Both parties understood that they were far smaller than the Leninist mass-parties that they believed were necessary to bring about revolution. But both believed that their parties could play the leading role in building such a party. The question they therefore faced was whether the moment of generalised working-class struggle had arrived that would precipitate the building of a mass party. This question permeated the debates over the future of the ULA.

Ultimately, both groups concluded that the ULA was too inchoate, and that it made more sense to work through their own growing organisations. The reason the SP gave for its reluctance to build the ULA was that it didn't see it as an effective vehicle to mobilise working-class struggle or even to mobilise electorally. In January 2012, the de-facto leader of the SP, Kevin McLoughlin, sounded the death knell for the ULA when writing, 'Moving to establish a party without the actual involvement of significant numbers of ordinary working-class people, would lead it to becoming an irrelevant political sect. The ULA is not the new party, nor is it likely to just become the new party at some future date.'[4] Actions followed words and the SP disengaged from the ULA, leaving it early the following year. The SWP, while publicly stating they wanted to build the ULA, sounded a different note in a leaked internal bulletin of 6 February 2012, which lambasted other groups in the alliance.[5] They relaunched PBP in summer 2012, signalling their own withdrawal from the ULA.

While the failure of the ULA was a blow to the left, there were substantive reasons why both parties were hostile to unity. One long-term SP activist, 'Mark P', derided the idea of unity for unity's sake as a form of 'magical thinking', pointing out that,

> pushing people with very hardened political views on top of each other to argue the toss over and over again without any wider set of participants who can both adjudicate and offer their

own alternative perspectives is likely to cause more ill will rather than ease it. It's the tie cats in a sack version of building left wing cooperation.[6]

The unanswered question remains though, if they had built the ULA, would that wider set of participants have arrived?

FEAR AND LOATHING – TROTSKYISTS AND THE REST OF THE LEFT

There is a good chance that they may not have attracted others, due to the problematic relationship that the Trotskyist parties had with other groups on the left, whether trade unions, other parties or simply people they'd worked with on campaigns. The mutual hostility vis-à-vis trade unions might seem difficult to understand initially, considering the importance both groups placed on organised activity in the workplace. But both parties were virulently critical of the union leadership for their moderation and allegiance to partnership arrangements. Instead, they favoured a strategy of confrontation with government and bosses and constantly criticised unions for selling out workers. However, they did little more than criticise, deprioritising trade union work in this period relative to community and electoral activities. There were a few initiatives with regards to union work, mainly supporting workers in dispute such as the Thomas Cook workers' sit-in, but there was nothing sustained. Even the SP, which had had the stronger working-class focus, decided against putting much effort into organising against the Croke Park agreements (see Chapter 6 on unions), something which disillusioned several of their trade union activists.[7] So even leftwing trade union activists tended to dismiss the Trotskyist parties as engaging in mere verbal leftism – calling for a general strike while only being involved in occasional union activities.

This stance of permanent opposition also affected their relations with potential voters and those on the social democratic left who felt that, while opposition parties should take oppositionalist stances, they should do something more – such as suggesting viable alternatives and potential halfway houses. The Trotskyist parties did nothing of this. Instead, they saw their role as exposing the limitations of capitalism, and simply offer criticism.

However, the political positioning of the Trotskyist parties doesn't by itself explain why large sections of the left were allergic to them. What soured relations was Trotskyist practices of organising within campaigns. With some differences, the practices of both parties were broadly similar. They sought to use campaigns to build a broader anti-capitalist movement. They did this by using their accumulated experience and political knowledge to push campaigns in a radical socialist direction, educating those less politically aware to think beyond the single issue they were campaigning on. As such, they stood against compromise with centrist and rightwing elements in campaigns, and encouraged campaigners to get involved in wider political life through the agency of the revolutionary party. Or, as it was often seen by non-Trotskyists, their repeated strategy was to establish a dominant position in campaigns, to engineer splits and crises against those who disagreed with their tactics – tactics seen as benefiting their parties rather than the campaign, to recruit members and leave the campaign once its capacity to build the party had been exhausted. There is little common ground between these two understandings of Trotskyist parties: as a political vanguard who sought to lead campaigns in order to further joined-up working-class revolutionary action, or as predators leeching off and splitting campaigns to maintain the churn of members their organisations worked through.

There were also differences in how the SWP and SP were viewed by other left activists. Broadly, the SWP was seen as dishonest, while the SP was seen as sectarian. Either way it meant that even the most innocuous of their actions were regarded with deep suspicion by those they worked with, or by others who refused to work with them. This suspicion was as much a factor as their frequently destructive actions in limiting their influence. One example of this was during the Occupy movement, when hostility to the SWP trying to take over the movement – whether or not they were actually trying to do so – spread to broader hostility against organised leftwing and trade union groups.

More enduring examples can be seen in the major campaigns of the period. After the collapse, or rather during the collapse, of the ULA, both parties sought to work through alternative alliances and electoral formations. The SP, having been possibly the leading organisers and largest formation in the Campaign Against Household and Water Taxes (CAHWT), had succeeded in their attempt to get the campaign to endorse candidates for the 2014 local elections (see Chapter 2). However, this was a pyrrhic victory. The tensions and disagreements in CAHWT, aggravated by its failure and the SP's attempts to push it towards electoralism, led to its collapse. Unable to use CAHWT as its electoral vehicle, the SP responded by forming the Anti-Austerity Alliance in February 2014. Using this new name, it won 14 seats in the local elections of that year.

However, their biggest victory was in the Dublin South West by-election in October 2014 when their candidate, Paul Murphy, pulled off a surprise victory over the heavily favoured Sinn Féin candidate, Cathal King. Murphy and the SP had focused heavily on the issue of water charges, claiming that Sinn Féin wouldn't meaningfully oppose them. This by-election upset did indeed push Sinn Féin towards a more outright opposition towards water charges than they'd shown towards household charges, and it was one of the events that helped galvanise the campaign in its early stages. For the SP, this victory vindicated their uncompromising stance, in particular their call for an outright boycott on water charges. They focused on this aspect of the campaign to the extent of suggesting that those organisations who didn't support a boycott shouldn't be allowed to participate in the Right2Water campaign – including the unions which funded Right2Water. As this didn't happen, the SP formed a Non-Payment Network through which it campaigned, which further opened up the distance between themselves and others.

This division meant that when the trade unions formed Right2Change, the SP did not take part. In itself, this wasn't perhaps that important, more that it indicated their isolation away from other anti-austerity campaigners. Right2Change was an attempt to form a progressive bloc off the back of the water charges victory in time for the 2016 elections. However, it failed to gain much traction, partly because it was even more inchoate than the ULA and also because it wasn't treated seriously by its constituent parts. Sinn Féin, for instance, viewed it more as a loose transfer pact than a serious alliance, saying the policy principles they signed up to were 'aims, rather than definitive commitments'.[8] The SP's long-standing opposition to Sinn Féin, combined with mutual hostility with the trade union leadership of Right2Change, excluded them from involvement.

Their strategy of forming their own organisation, rather than cooperate with other groups, was also used during the abortion campaign. They set up ROSA in 2013 as a vehicle to bring young feminist women into the party and campaign for abortion, separately from other groups. While some within the party and many outside it criticised it as a sectarian front group which refused to work with the Abortion Rights Campaign, ROSA proved successful in its own terms, recruiting members into the SP and pushing the party towards a more feminist intersectional approach in their politics, although this was something that would carry problems for them later.

Meanwhile, the SWP sought with greater success to work through PBP. Rather than staying outside the room as the SP increasingly did, they worked within existing campaigns. For instance, unlike the SP, they signed up to the Right2Change principles, advocating a transfer pact with others on the left. At the same time, one shouldn't overstate the difference between the parties. As Oisín Vince Coulter explains, in the water charges campaign, both the SWP and SP 'marshalled the tactics of the united front, nominally working alongside the others while trying to outflank them by being more radical'.[9] Even though the SWP had a more conciliatory approach to other groups, they still formed different offshoots, working both within and outside campaigns. One example is in the case of Palestine – an issue on which they remained centrally active throughout the period. Although, they did work with the broad Ireland Palestine Solidarity Campaign, they also formed a separate group, Action for Palestine, as well as working through the Irish Anti-War Movement, which they effectively controlled. To add to the confusion and distrust, they would also call rival events and demonstrations on behalf of PBP and, less frequently, the SWP.

PBP was becoming more than an electoral front group for the SWP, or as they would put it, an electoral alliance in which they were the main component. The party was moving out of student societies into a more sustained engagement with working-class communities and the electorate. At their February 2018 conference, the leadership of the SWP decided to dissolve the SWP as a distinct party. Instead, they launched the Socialist Worker Network (SWN) as a faction within PBP, declaring that in future they would operate through this group. While a surprising move, it made sense in the context of seeking to break out of a small cohort of like-minded party adherents and gain greater public traction. The entry of Paul Murphy's grouping RISE into PBP in 2021 helped their claim that PBP was more than the SWP. However, the SWN remains the dominant faction within PBP and many continue to see it as a SWN/P front group.

SPLITS AND CONTINUATIONS

While the relative success of the SWP's electoralist front led the party to dissolve into it, the success of the SP's feminist front group, ROSA, had a more damaging if unintentional knock-on effect on the fortunes of the party, precipitating a series of events that led to its split and collapse. The problem as such was the success of ROSA in reorienting the SP towards feminist campaigning. This provided critics of the SP within the UK-dominated international parent group, the Committee for a Workers International (CWI), the opportunity to attack the SP for abandoning working-class struggle in favour of identity politics and culture wars.

Peter Taaffe, the long-term de-facto leader of the CWI and in particular its UK section, the Socialist Party in England and Wales (SPEW), issued a ten-page document denouncing 'some leading Irish comrades' for 'seeing all struggles through the prism of the women's movement, rather than seeing how it interconnects with other struggles' and cautioned them not to 'adopt wholesale the language of petit-bourgeois feminism'.[10] Behind this criticism lay sharp differences between the Irish and English parties on Sinn Féin, with the SP taking a far more critical approach to the possibility of a Sinn Féin-led government than SPEW.[11]

In its response the Irish organisation rejected the charges.[12] Somewhat inevitably the disagreement became a split, not simply between the British and Irish groups or in the wider CWI, but within these groups as well. Within the SP, three factions were formed – the so-called Non-Faction Faction, which comprised most of the party's leadership; a much smaller faction which agreed with Taaffe's attack on the Irish party; and finally Transform the Party. This faction, headed by Paul Murphy TD, rejected Taaffe's sectarianism while agreeing with some of the criticism of the Irish party, mainly advocating for a more open approach vis-à-vis other left groups, particularly Sinn Féin. Paul Murphy moulded this faction into an autonomous grouping, RISE, when he left the much-depleted SP in September 2019.[13] He later joined PBP with his group in February 2021, widening the electoral gulf between the two parties.

Behind the disagreements in the SP lay serious organisational weaknesses. The British section claimed that the SP only had 100 members. While this may be a deliberate undercount, even the SP's boast that the influence of ROSA enabled it to recruit 35 members in the whole of 2018 was a claim that reveals the tiny membership base of the party. It also revealed their reliance on TDs' salaries; despite their tiny membership, they had 19 full-time and ten part-time staff in 2019. With the defection of Paul Murphy and the loss of Ruth Coppinger's seat, this became unsustainable. But even before the party imploded, it was notable that the large number of staff did not affect the limited reach of a party who many people found they could not work with. While PBP had a larger membership base and greater electoral success, the problem of distrust also limited their reach. Nevertheless they managed to weather the storm of Sinn Féin's success in 2020 to better effect than their rivals and allies in the SP.

Also, in contrast with the SP's problems with its British mother party, PBP/SWP was remarkably unaffected by the 2013–14 rape scandal in the British SWP.[14] While the British SWP was convulsed over the issue, losing much of its membership and credibility, the Irish organisation successfully distanced themselves from the scandal, adopting a position of saying little, but condemning the British organisation when asked about it.

CONCLUSION

It is difficult to imagine any campaign of the era without the contribution of the two Trotskyist parties. They provided an enthusiastic, if constantly fluctuating, cadre of volunteers, as well as seasoned leadership to undertake the essential work of leafleting, postering, holding stalls and local meetings, providing speakers and publicising these causes to the utmost of their abilities. They organised demonstrations and blocs at demonstrations around the country. They were not of course the only groups to do this, but they were an essential part of campaigns, in many areas providing leadership and vision to the anti-austerity movement. They also 'held the line' when it came to campaigning – challenging social democrats and opposing compromises in both outcomes and campaigning and constantly pushing for disruptive rather than polite actions to tackle austerity, for instance, leading the calls for non-payment in the campaign against the water tax.

To a certain extent, they benefited from their activities and prominence. Leading members such as Richard Boyd-Barrett, Paul Murphy, Bríd Smith and Ruth Coppinger achieved media standing and electoral success. The parties' success went beyond these figures. At their height in 2016 they had six TDs and 28 councillors elected. But there was a ceiling to this success. Despite all their efforts they failed to fully capitalise on their campaigning, and never came near building a mass party of the working class or even an electoral vehicle that went significantly beyond their small organisations. Rather, the SP imploded with the infighting common to ideologically driven groups. The more flexible SWP did better, folding itself into its electoral vehicle, PBP, and maintaining both a presence in the Dáil and local authorities in Dublin, as well as a strong presence in leftwing campaigns. But distrust of the party, especially by those who have worked with them, continues to muffle their effect and limit them. However, even if the recession was not the occasion for them to break through and establish a mass party, they have managed to persist. This in itself may be counted as a success.

NOTES

1. PBP's main recruit was Joan Collins, a former SP community activist in the working-class areas of Crumlin and Drimnagh. Her Community and Workers Action Group joined PBP in 2007 and she was one of the two TDs elected in 2009. However, she left the group in 2013.

2. Thus, PBP more or less avoided west Dublin and Limerick, where AAA was strong, and AAA in turn didn't contest many seats in south county and city Dublin where PBP candidates polled well.

3. Socialist Workers Party, 'After the United Left Alliance Forum', 27 June 2011; Socialist Party, 'What Program for the United Left Alliance? – After the ULA Forum: Which Way Forward?", 14 July 2011.

4. Kevin McLoughlin, 'What Next for the United Left Alliance', 17 January 2012, https://tinyurl.com/ynuhw6wv (all URLs last accessed 24 June 2024).

5. Tomás Ó Flatharta, 'Kubla Heard from Far: The Problem with the ULA Is Everybody Else', 9 February 2012, https://tinyurl.com/2h6v2zn2.

6. Mark P., 'On the One Hand on the Other Hand on the One Hand', 31 January 2013, https://tinyurl.com/4awkra3m.

7. Andrew Phelan, Megan Ni Ghabhlain, Richard O'Hara, Pamela Rochford, Stephanie O'Shea and Jimmy Dignam, 'Socialist Party Resignation Statement', 19 December 2013, https://tinyurl.com/2s43uteh.

8. Fiach Kelly, 'Sinn Féin to Agree Pact with Left-Wing Parties and Independents', *Irish Times*, 27 October 2015.

9. Oisín Vince Coulter, 'The PBP/Solidarity Explainer: From Campaigns to Revolution', *Village Magazine*, 6 February 2020, https://villagemagazine.ie/the-pbp-solidarity-explainer-from-campaigns-to-revolution/.

10. International Secretariat, 'Women's Oppression and Identity Politics, Our Approach in Ireland and Internationally', November 2018, https://tinyurl.com/hj6wv7zf.

11. Irish NEC Majority, 'Setting the Record Straight a Response to the IS Majority and Platform Statement – Part 1', 10 December 2019, https://tinyurl.com/2jvmkwem.

12. NEC in Ireland, 'A Response to the IS document, "Women's Oppression and Identity Politics – Our Approach in Ireland and Internationally"', November 2018.

13. The 'non-faction faction' in the SP retained control of the party. With the split in their parent body, they joined CWI-Majority, renamed in 2020 as International Socialist Alternative. The small pro-Taaffe group in Ireland became Militant Left. Their parent body retains the name, CWI.

14. Edward Platt, 'Comrades at War: The Decline and Fall of the Socialist Workers Party', *New Statesman*, 20 May 2014, https://tinyurl.com/534y5sm3.

10

Republicanism

Dan Finn, Stewart Reddin and Damian Lawlor

The trajectories of Sinn Féin and the smaller militant republican groups were dramatically different during the years of austerity. Firstly, there is the issue of size. While Sinn Féin does not comprise the entirety of contemporary Irish republicanism, it is far bigger than all the other tendencies. This has meant that it faces different issues and has gone in different directions to its smaller rivals.

During this period, Sinn Féin was grappling with the question of entering government in Dublin and how to appeal to a broader base of voters. It had an ambiguous relationship with social movements and anti-austerity campaigning, offering qualified support and benefitting from these campaigns, but maintaining a certain distance. In contrast, socialist republican groups – Éirígí in particular – embraced anti-austerity campaigning, especially during the early years of the economic crisis. However, despite their energy and activism, their message didn't connect with the broader public and they failed to reap the rewards of their actions.

This chapter examines these very different groups separately, firstly looking at the smaller left republican groups and then Sinn Féin, as well as considering the reasons for and results of their different trajectories.

MILITANT REPUBLICANISM DURING
THE AUSTERITY YEARS

The 2004 local and European elections represented a significant point in Sinn Féin's electoral advance in the 26 counties. The party more than doubled its local representation from 21 to 54 seats, while its share of the vote increased from 3.6 per cent in the 1999 local elections to 8 per cent in 2004. It performed particularly well in working-class areas of Dublin and in border counties of Monaghan, Louth and Donegal. Its campaign in Dublin also saw the party elect its first MEP, with Mary Lou McDonald securing 14 per cent of the vote.

The mainstream media considered Sinn Féin's success as reward for years of community activism, particularly in working-class areas of the capital. Sinn Féin, despite being the oldest party in the state, was considered the 'new kid on the block', with the energy, resolve and resources to become a significant electoral force in the 26 counties. The prospect of it holding the balance of power at the next general election in the South was, however, to generate tensions within the party. *An Phoblacht* reported on the Dublin Sinn Féin AGM in February 2006, which was addressed by Martin McGuinness. He expressed confidence that Sinn Féin was on the road to becoming the largest nationalist party in the six counties, but that this would be 'as of nothing' if the party did not do the same in the South. Reports at the AGM that Sinn Féin was aiming to become the largest party in Dublin were, he said, 'speaking his language'.[1]

However, the ebullient nature of the Dublin Sinn Féin in February 2006 masked internal tensions within the organisation. It appeared the prospect of securing power in the South as a junior coalition partner with the centre-right Fianna Fáil party was something the party leadership was willing to countenance. Within months of the AGM, a small number of activists in Dublin left the party and formed a new socialist republican campaigning group, Éirígí.

This party was to prove both a challenge to Sinn Féin and a means of mobilising leftwing republicans to fight the oncoming austerity programme of the Irish government. However, it failed to build on its initial momentum, and by 2012 was experiencing divisions that would diminish and demoralise the organisation.

The activists who formed Éirígí claimed that the Sinn Féin leadership was abandoning leftwing policies in order to make itself acceptable as a coalition partner to Fianna Fáil. At its first Ard Fheis, in 2007, Éirígí declared itself a 'revolutionary political party'.[2] Over the following months several high-profile speakers addressed Éirígí commemorations in Dublin, including former civil rights leader Bernadette McAliskey and leading Belfast republican and former hunger-striker Bernard Fox. Éirígí's assessment that Sinn Féin's courting of a coalition with Fianna Fáil would result in a loss of support in working-class communities proved prescient. Despite predictions of significant gains, Sinn Féin won less than 7 per cent of the vote and returned with just four seats, one less than the previous general election in 2002. An apparent halt to Sinn Féin's electoral advance, alongside the energy and growth displayed by Éirígí in its first year, led the latter's chairperson, Brian Leeson, to boldly declare:

> Much has been said and written in recent times about the state of the republican struggle. Éirígí is ready to play its part in rejuvenating the struggle and looks forward with optimism and hope to doing so. We intend not only to radically redefine the nature of Irish society but also the struggle to achieve that change.[3]

The accuracy of that assessment would be tested over the following years. Éirígí played an active role in the defeat of the Lisbon Treaty referendum that summer and, while it did not contest the 2009 local elections in the South, the election provided the party with its first elected representative when Sinn Féin councillor Louise Minihan joined Éirígí. In a subsequent interview with Dan Keenan of the *Irish Times*, Brian Leeson claimed, 'with a proven track record of political campaigning, combined with an unambiguous socialist republican platform the party was attracting large numbers of existing left wing republicans'.[4]

Following the 2008 global financial crash, Éirígí believed the austerity programme instigated by the Irish government offered it an opportunity to become the voice of militant socialist republicanism. The Irish establishment view of who should pay the price for the banking crisis was set out in the McCarthy report, which proposed swingeing cuts of €5.3 billion to public services and social welfare rates, along with a recommendation to introduce domestic water charges.[5] Éirígí argued that this would lead to the gutting of the public sector and economic devastation for the most vulnerable in Irish society. The budget proposals were considered a declaration of war on the working class, with a response in kind required. Over the following years, Éirígí would provide an energetic street-level opposition to the cuts.

Éirígí appeared to be preparing for a sustained campaign against the Irish government's austerity measures. It launched its 'Smash the NAMA Republic' campaign in April producing leaflets, stickers and a satirical version of the 1916 Proclamation, the 'NAMA Proclamation', which declared the right of private banks to the ownership of Ireland.[6] Impatient with what it considered the lack of a robust challenge to the Irish government's austerity programme, it declared the time for 'quiet talking and polite debate had passed. The time for action is upon us.'[7]

An example of this was the occupation of Anglo Irish Bank. This was the favoured bank of Ireland's property developers. Its reckless lending practices during the boom years of the Celtic Tiger led to the banking crisis that ultimately sank the economy in 2008. The Irish government bailed out the bank to the tune of €30 billion, the equivalent of 20 per cent of Ireland's GDP at the time. At 7.00 a.m. on 15 May 2010, four Éirígí activists climbed on to the roof of Anglo Irish Bank on Dublin's Stephen's Green and unfurled a banner proclaiming, 'People of Ireland, Rise Up'. The slogan was inspired by a demonstration in Greece the previous week when activists from the Greek Communist Party occupied the Acropolis in Athens and dropped a banner calling on the peoples of Europe to rise up in opposition to austerity.[8]

While a large crowd gathered outside the bank in support of the activists, where an effigy of Anglo Irish's chief executive, Seán Fitzpatrick, was hung, Gardaí removed windows from the upper stories of the building and attempted to violently pull the activists, who had chained themselves together, from the roof. As those on the ground objected to this heavy-handed approach, Gardaí waded into the crowd with batons. Six people were arrested. In a defiant statement, an Éirígí spokesperson declared it was 'send[ing] a message to the business class and their servants in Leinster House that they can no longer get away with their acts of theft without facing the direct action of any angry and united people'.[9]

Throughout 2010, demonstrations against austerity intensified. In mid-May, the *Sunday Independent* reported that Gardaí were training in secret for riots, amidst 'fears of Greek-style violence stirred in wake of Dáil attack by protestors'.[10] This was in reference to a brief scuffle outside the Irish parliament when a small number of protestors, including Éirígí members, attempted to storm the gates. Gardaí drew batons and several protestors were injured. A similar protest the following week involving members of Éirígí, and other leftwing and republican groups drew the ire of the *Evening Herald*, castigating what it termed the 'ugly face of republicanism', which had 'cast a shadow over Dublin city centre'.[11] On this occasion, a large force of Gardaí, several on horseback, and backed up by the Garda riot squad, created an impenetrable barrier to the Dáil for the relatively small numbers gathered in protest.

As the anti-austerity campaign gathered momentum and Éirígí's public profile grew, the party suddenly shifted focus and instead concentrated its effort and resources over the following six months into a campaign against the proposed visit to Ireland of the British monarch. Meanwhile, militant republicans, who heretofore had been silent on the devastating impact of the Europe-wide austerity programme on the working class, began to find their voice. In the latter part of the 2000s, groups such as the Real Irish Republican Army (RIRA) and Óglaigh na hÉireann (ONH) were emerging from a period of reorganisation. However, as the global financial crisis deepened in early 2009, there were no signs that these militant republicans were focused on the emerging movement resisting austerity. In the Easter statement issued by republican prisoners associated with the RIRA, there was no mention of the banking crisis or the social unrest that was developing. While the statement finished with the words, 'we remain steadfast in our pursuit of the 32 County Socialist Republic', these militant republicans were not offering a coherent socialist analysis of the developing crisis.

However, by September 2010, there was a dramatic shift in that organisation's focus. In an interview with *The Guardian*, the RIRA described bankers as criminals and stated its intention to launch attacks against 'military, political and economic targets'. It claimed that this was consistent with past tactics, 'We have a track record of attacking high-profile economic targets and financial institutions such as the City of London. The role of bankers and the institutions they serve in financing Britain's colonial and capitalist system has not gone unnoticed.'[12]

Three weeks after this interview, the RIRA exploded a 200 lb bomb at an Ulster Bank branch in Derry. Sinn Féin's Martin McGuinness, addressing a fringe meeting of the British Conservative Party conference, denounced the attack as 'the futile activities of these conflict junkies.'[13] In October 2011 the RIRA claimed responsibility for a number of attacks on banks, including the Ulster Bank bomb in October 2010, as well as attacks on Santander bank branches in Derry and Newry in summer of 2011. The RIRA claimed the attacks were intended to 'send out the message that while the Irish national and class struggles are distinct, they are not separate.'[14]

Éirígí in turn placed itself firmly within the revolutionary Marxist tradition in its late 2010 policy paper, *From Socialism Alone Can the Salvation of Ireland Come*. The paper contained a swipe at those within the Irish republican tradition who subordinated the struggle for social and economic rights to the struggle for national rights. Éirígí asserted that this represented,

A fundamentally flawed and reactionary position, which has often led to the struggle for 'Ireland' being elevated in importance above, and as something distinct from, the struggle for the interests of the people of Ireland. There can be no compromise between the capitalist class and the working class, or any question of separating out the question of national liberation from that of class conflict.[15]

In the build-up to the Irish government's December budget in 2010, Éirígí published a detailed analysis of the government's austerity plan, warning that the budget would see 'the working class sacrificed upon the altar of "competitiveness" while our public services are to be plundered in the interests of international investment capital'. It concluded, 'a sustained and relentless class war has been underway for some time and must be met with equally vigorous and determined action'.[16] In early November, Éirígí's 'vigorous and determined action' came in the form of an attack on Minister for Health, Mary Harney, during an event at Cherry Orchard hospital in Ballyfermot. Local Éirígí councillor Louise Minihan poured a bottle of red paint over Harney's clothing, representing, as she claimed, 'the blood that she and the rest of the Dublin government have on their hands as a result of the cutbacks to healthcare'.[17] Minihan was later found guilty of assault and criminal damage, receiving a two-month suspended prison sentence and €1,500 fine. Just days after the Harney incident Éirígí was once again the focus of media attention, this time accused of 'hijacking' a student protest in Dublin against increases to the third level student registration fee.[18] A section of the estimated 40,000 crowd broke from the main body of the demonstration and occupied the Department of Finance offices. Gardaí in riot gear violently ejected those occupying the building, leading to clashes on the street outside and three arrests.

The first half of 2011 saw Éirígí focus exclusively on its campaign against the state visit to Ireland of the British monarch. The party was the primary organising force against the visit but failed to mobilise significant numbers to its various demonstrations, or to draw other forces into its campaign. The Irish state put on a massive show of force, mobilising an estimated 8,000 Gardaí during the visit. While Éirígí maintained an active presence during the following years of the anti-austerity campaign, it failed to match the energy it displayed in 2010.

The party was affiliated to the Campaign Against Household and Water Taxes, formally launched in December 2011. Several of its members played an active role on the campaign steering committee and in the organisation of a mass public meeting attended by thousands in the National Stadium in Dublin in March 2012. A campaign demonstration at the Labour Party conference in Galway in April saw Garda lines broken by protestors who attempted to gain access to the hotel. Media reports again emphasised the presence of Éirígí.[19] However, organisational cracks had begun to emerge in the summer of 2012. The party's high-profile public representative in Donegal, Mícheál Mac Giolla Easbuig, left the party.

The party ran six candidates in the 2014 local elections in the 26 counties, two of whom were sitting councillors, Louise Minihan in Dublin and John Dwyer in Wexford. (Dwyer had joined Éirígí in 2012 as a sitting Sinn Féin councillor.)[20] However, both performed poorly and lost their seats. The party's other candidates failed to make an impact. Its former representative in Donegal, MacGiolla Easbuig, ran as an independent candidate and won a seat in the Glenties electoral area. While the water tax campaign provided much needed focus for the party from late 2014 into 2015, it was clear by that point it had lost momentum.

Between 2016 and 2017, significant fractures emerged. The founding of Saoradh in 2016 saw members in both Dublin and Newry defect to the new party. Meanwhile the entire membership of Éirígí in the south-east left to form Anti-Imperialist Action Ireland, while party members in Belfast left *en-masse* to form a new group, Lasair Dhearg. By this time neither of its former councillors, Louise Minihan or John Dwyer, were members of the party. Éirígí ran just three candidates in the 2019 local elections in the 26 counties, failing to win a seat. By 2020, two of its three 2019 local election candidates had left the party, and its public profile had plummeted. Éirígí had no active branches in the six counties and only a scattering of members in the South. Almost all of those who had been members of Éirígí in the first five years of its existence, when the party's profile and activity was at its zenith, had left. Meanwhile, Sinn Féin, the organisation it left in 2006, and which was floundering at the polls in 2007, was on the cusp of taking state power in the South.

SINN FÉIN – READY FOR GOVERNMENT?

Between 2007 and 2020, Sinn Féin went from being a minor force in the political system south of the Irish border to become the largest party in the state, with a vote share exceeding that of Fine Gael, Fianna Fáil or Labour. The main factor behind this rise was the economic crisis that followed the crash of 2008, which offered Sinn Féin new opportunities to challenge and eventually surpass the formerly dominant political actors in the South. However, the party's electoral growth did not follow a smooth, unbroken trajectory during this period: at one point, it appeared to be facing a sharp decline in its fortunes, before unexpectedly bouncing back to reach a new peak. Nor did Sinn Féin itself follow a consistent strategy: the party leadership changed its view on such basic questions as the idea of forming a coalition government with the centre-right parties more than once.

Sinn Féin went into the 2007 general election with high hopes for a breakthrough. The party's vice-president, Pat Doherty, announced that Sinn Féin was 'preparing to be in government, north and south' and expected to 'substantially increase our representation in constituencies right across the country'.[21] The leader of Sinn Féin's Dáil group, Caoimhghín Ó Caoláin, pledged that republicans would 'prioritise the provision of public services for all on the basis of equality' if they joined a governing coalition, while Dublin MEP Mary Lou McDonald said that increased social expenditure should come before tax cuts.[22] On the eve of the election, Adams predicted that the party was going to receive a 'very, very big vote', supplying it with a 'mandate for government'.[23]

The result on 24 May thus came as a bitter disappointment. The party increased its vote share slightly, from 6.5 to 6.9 per cent, but it did not win any new seats. In fact, one of the five TDs who had been elected in 2002, Seán Crowe, lost his seat in Dublin South-West. There was no question of Sinn Féin imposing itself as a necessary coalition partner on the traditional governing parties in the South. In a post-election interview, Gerry Adams acknowledged that there had been 'very high, and often unrealistic expectations about seat gains' during the run up to the vote.[24]

Sinn Féin's Ard Chomhairle discussed the setback in June, with several speakers stressing the need to 'develop Southern leadership' and find ways of making the party's republicanism 'relevant to people within the objective conditions pertaining in the 26 Counties'.[25] Speaking at Bodenstown a few weeks later, Adams referred to the challenges with which Sinn Féin had to grapple as a party 'operating in two jurisdictions with their own political cultures and different political realities that have developed since partition'. He insisted that those challenges were not insurmountable: 'We have entered a new phase of our struggle. While we must continue to advance in the North the front line is now clearly shifting South.'[26]

In December 2007, Sinn Féin held a special conference under the banner 'Engaging Modern Ireland'. Some of the comments made by Adams hinted at a move towards the economic centre ground:

'We need to be as comfortable with words like "prosperity" and "economic opportunity" as we are with "equality" and "independence".'[27] At the party's Ard Fheis in March 2008, he stressed that the party's economic policy was 'pro-business'.[28] But the immediate priority was the forthcoming referendum on the EU's Lisbon Treaty. The Irish Greens had campaigned against the Nice Treaty in 2001 and 2002. However, after joining a Fianna Fáil-led coalition in the wake of the 2007 election, they opted to endorse Lisbon, leaving Sinn Féin as the only party in the Dáil to oppose it. Mary Lou McDonald argued that it was 'possible to support the EU and be against the Lisbon Treaty' and summarised the party's objections to the document:

> It gives the EU too much power and reduces our ability to stop decisions that are not in Ireland's interests. It cuts our voting strength on the Council of Ministers by more than half and ends our automatic right to a Commissioner. It erodes neutrality. It allows the EU to act in the international arena in the same way as a state and to form a diplomatic corps. It seriously undermines workers' rights and public services, and it is bad for the developing world.[29]

The 'No' vote on 12 June, by a margin of 53.4 to 46.6 per cent on a 53 per cent turnout, thus came as a boon to Sinn Féin after the disappointments of the previous year. There was to be a second Lisbon plebiscite in October 2009, with Sinn Féin once again calling for a 'No' vote, this time unsuccessfully. By then, however, the main focus of public debate in the South had shifted to the crisis that unfolded after the collapse of Lehman Brothers in autumn 2008.

After the Crash

The economic meltdown and its long-term fall-out proved to be the making of Sinn Féin as a major force in southern politics, although the party's initial response to the government's handling of the crisis was rather tentative. When Finance Minister Brian Lenihan announced a state guarantee for the private banking sector soon after the crash, Sinn Féin's Dáil representatives supported the necessary legislation – albeit with 'concerns and reservations', according to Caoimhghín Ó Caoláin.[30] This gave the Labour Party space to outflank its main leftwing challenger by opposing the legislation outright.

Sinn Féin did not make the same mistake twice. As the crisis steadily worsened, its TDs consistently opposed the moves made by Lenihan and his colleagues, from the nationalisation of Anglo Irish Bank to the creation of the National Asset Management Agency (NAMA), which bought up the distressed assets of developers at a price above their market value.[31] Opposing the bill to establish NAMA, Ó Caoláin told the Dáil that his party wanted the government to nationalise the two main private financial institutions, Bank of Ireland and Allied Irish Bank, and turn them into a state bank with which to manage the crisis.[32]

At the Sinn Féin Ard Fheis in February 2009, Gerry Adams called for 'a new alliance of all people and parties that want real and fundamental change' and urged Labour to join it: 'The Labour Party has a duty not to prop up either Fianna Fáil or Fine Gael.'[33] Mary Lou McDonald drove home the message two months later:

> Change won't come by replacing a failed Fianna Fáil-led government with a Fine Gael-led coalition. We need more than just new faces at the Cabinet table. To create long-term, sustainable and equitable economic recovery we need a fundamental change of values and of social and economic policies. This is something that neither Fianna Fáil nor Fine Gael can offer.[34]

The government led by Fianna Fáil's Brian Cowen held on until the beginning of 2011, when it collapsed soon after Ireland was forced to enter the bailout programme of the EU–ECB–IMF 'Troika', along with Greece and Portugal.

Sinn Féin entered the general election campaign with a burst of momentum from a long-delayed by-election in Donegal South-West: the party's candidate Pearse Doherty received almost 40 per cent of first-preference votes – more than his opponents from Fianna Fáil and Fine Gael put together. The broad left, from Labour to the Trotskyists of the United Left Alliance (ULA), all made gains in the election, and Sinn Féin was no exception: the party's vote share rose by 3 per cent and its parliamentary group increased from four TDs in 2007 to 14. Gerry Adams had vacated his traditional base in West Belfast to spearhead the party's southern strategy from Louth, where he topped the poll. Adams was joined by Doherty, re-elected in Donegal, and Mary Lou McDonald also entered the Dáil for the first time, representing Dublin Central, although Eoin Ó Broin fell short of taking a seat in Dublin Mid-West. Over the next decade, McDonald, Doherty and Ó Broin would form the core of a new leadership team based south of the border, all of whom had become active in the party since the peace process began, in contrast with veterans such as Ó Caoláin, Crowe or Kerry's Martin Ferris.

In the short term, however, the main beneficiary of a leftwards shift in popular opinion was the Labour Party, which took almost 20 per cent of the vote, overtaking Fianna Fáil for the first time. This presented the Labour leadership with a fateful choice. They could have turned down the opportunity to enter government and set out to form a leftwing alliance from the opposition benches. In that scenario, Fine Gael would almost certainly have formed a minority government with support or cooperation from a much-diminished Fianna Fáil, which had just lost 51 of its 71 seats. The *Irish Times* columnist Stephen Collins reflected on the likely outcome of this alternative strategy after the next general election in 2016:

> [Labour] could have stayed out of government and allowed Fine Gael to try and govern on its own. After all, Fine Gael was not too far off an overall majority and nobody was in much doubt that it would proceed to implement the broad outline of the policies put in place by the previous Fianna Fáil government. That would have allowed Labour the luxury of opposition and it would probably have emerged as the biggest party by now.[35]

Instead, Labour opted for the traditional path of forming a government as Fine Gael's junior partner, having resisted Sinn Féin's overtures to join an 'alliance for change'. This meant accepting the Troika's austerity policies which it had recently stigmatised on the campaign trial with slogans like 'Labour's way or Frankfurt's way'.

The electoral consequences for Labour proved to be devastating five years later.

'Fundamental Change'

For Sinn Féin, the fruits of Labour's fateful choice were mixed. On the one hand, it left the way clear for Adams and his colleagues to position themselves as the main opponents of austerity throughout a period in which the Fine Gael–Labour coalition pushed through major cuts to public spending that compounded the impact of the Great Recession on working-class living standards. Neither the Trotskyists of the ULA, which broke up soon after the 2011 election, nor the eclectic cohort of leftwing independents could hope to compete with Sinn Féin as a party with an established network of candidates and campaigners throughout the state. On the other hand, Labour's decision to coalesce with Fine Gael effectively meant that there was no prospect of a broad-left alliance forming a government after the next general election. Sinn Féin and the forces with which it might combine would have too much ground to make up in a single bound, so it would take at least two election cycles to make a leftwing government in Dublin a viable proposition.

While the question of economic policy dominated the lifetime of the next parliament, the period also saw the beginning of a major social movement to overturn the constitutional ban on abortion after the death of Savita Halappanavar in October 2012. For Sinn Féin, this was a sensitive topic: after the 1985 Ard Fheis adopted a pro-choice line, against the wishes of the party leadership, Gerry Adams successfully argued for that line to be dropped, telling supporters that it would 'weaken the overall thrust of the movement towards national freedom'.[36] There was little appetite in the party for a sudden change of direction.

In the wake of Halappanavar's death, Sinn Féin TDs called for legislation to put the X Case ruling of 1992 into effect, which would allow abortions to be carried out in Irish hospitals if the mother's life was in danger. Caoimhghín Ó Caoláin acknowledged that there were some party members who opposed this stance and described abortion as 'a most contentious issue with widely differing and sincerely held views'.[37] The 2015 Ard Fheis voted to support the legalisation of abortion in cases of fatal foetal abnormalities.[38] By the time the 2018 referendum was held, Sinn Féin supported outright repeal of the ban on abortion.[39] A vigorous pro-choice campaign had already done most of the work in terms of shifting public opinion before Sinn Féin changed its policy. The cautious handling of abortion rights was reflective of the party's general approach to social movements, where it was reluctant to stake out bold positions or function as a direct channel for those movements into mainstream politics.

As an alternative to the government's austerity policies, Sinn Féin put forward a neo-Keynesian, social-democratic agenda based on the expansion of public provision as its alternative. This raised the question of what political forces might be assembled around such an agenda. In the 2014 European election, Sinn Féin took 19.5 per cent of the vote, placing it within touching distance of Fine Gael and Fianna Fáil, both of which received 22.3 per cent. The following March, the party's Ard Fheis voted to rule out entering government as a junior partner with either of the traditional governing parties. Eoin Ó Broin, who had previously criticised Sinn Féin's drift towards the centre ground after the 2007 election result, told delegates that it was a question of fundamental importance:

For the first time in generations, we have the opportunity to break the Fianna Fáil/Fine Gael stranglehold on Southern politics. Decades of corruption, incompetence and greed can be brought to an end. The two-tier economy and society perpetuated by Mícheál Martin, Enda Kenny and Joan Burton can be transformed. We can start to build an Ireland of equals; a united Ireland; a better, fairer Ireland. But this can only happen if Sinn Féin makes a clear and unambiguous statement that we will not – under any circumstances – support a government led by Fianna Fáil or Fine Gael.[40]

Pearse Doherty made a similar argument as he promised that Sinn Féin would deliver 'fundamental change' if it entered government: 'We have no interest in propping up failed parties for the benefit of ministerial positions. That is what the Labour Party is for.'[41]

This fed into a wider debate on the Irish left, stemming from the campaign against water charges, which developed into the biggest anti-austerity social movement since the 2008 crash.[42] Mirroring their experience with the pro-choice movement, Sinn Féin was initially outflanked by the Trotskyist parties on the issue, who had put forward a call for mass non-payment of the charges. Paul Murphy of the Anti-Austerity Alliance edged past the Sinn Féin candidate Cathal King in a by-election held in Dublin South-West in October 2014. Some of the trade unions that had endorsed the Right-2Water campaigning front, including Unite and Mandate, later supported an effort to bring together the groups involved in the struggle against water charges around a wider policy platform.[43] The Right2Change initiative attracted support from Sinn Féin, People Before Profit and a number of leftwing independents in the 2016 election, although the Anti-Austerity Alliance refused to participate.[44]

From Athens to Dublin

The call for a 'progressive government' inevitably gave rise to questions about Sinn Féin's attitude towards the European Union. Having formerly called for outright withdrawal, the party now supported Irish EU membership while remaining sharply critical of the policies that were being promoted at a European level.[45] With the EU playing a much more intrusive role in domestic affairs than had been the case before the crisis, Sinn Féin had to formulate its response. The party called for a 'No' vote in a referendum on the EU's new fiscal treaty in May 2012, with Gerry Adams suggesting that it would hand power to 'unelected EU officials who cannot be removed by us, even if their decisions plunge us into more misery now and for generations to come'.[46]

Sinn Féin sought allies in other EU member states for its anti-austerity line and took a keen interest in the rise of Syriza, which formed a government in Greece at the beginning of 2015. An editorial in the party newspaper *An Phoblacht* described the Greek election as 'a vote for hope over fear'.[47] In the summer of 2015, Eoin Ó Broin reported from Athens after Syriza caved in to pressure from the Troika and the leading EU states to accept a new austerity programme. He described the general thrust of conversations with leading members of Syriza on their negotiations with the EU:

> People at all levels genuinely believed that rational arguments at the European Council could and would prevail. Their experience, however, had left their faith in the idea of an EU of equals badly shaken. One senior activist close to the negotiations spoke about how, week after week, their 'partners' kept moving the goalposts. Within a few months it became clear that their EU neither wanted to negotiate nor to secure a deal – they were intent on imposing a humiliating defeat.[48]

Ó Broin raised the question of whether it was possible to pursue an alternative economic policy within the framework of the Eurozone, without committing to the idea of a rupture:

> Greece, like Ireland, has long been one of the strongest advocates of the EU and Eurozone. But the standing of the EU institutions has taken a battering among ordinary Greek people. Though Greek society may not be prepared to exit the single currency just yet, even those on the most pro-EU wing of SYRIZA are now asking themselves whether they would be better off outside the euro. The only conclusion that can be drawn with any certainty in regard to recent events in Brussels and Athens is that the crisis of the Eurozone is far from over.[49]

Sinn Féin's opponents in the Irish government followed the unfolding drama in Greece with 'quiet satisfaction', according to Fiach Kelly of the *Irish Times*.[50] However, there was nothing quiet about the taunt delivered by Labour's Brendan Howlin as his Fine Gael colleague Michael Noonan presented the next year's budget in October 2015: 'Who speaks of Syriza now?' The *Irish Examiner* journalist Shaun Connolly compared Howlin's intervention to that of 'an angry child poking a wounded dog with a stick'.[51]

In the 2016 general election, Sinn Féin won twice as many votes as Labour, inverting the balance of 2011 between the parties. In other respects, however, the outcome came as a disappointment to Sinn Féin. Its vote share of 13.8 per cent was six points lower than its average polling score in 2015, and a late surge in support for Fianna Fáil during the campaign opened up a double-digit gap between the two parties which claimed the banner of republicanism. The idea that Sinn Féin might form a government with Fianna Fáil as its junior partner appeared to be slipping out of reach.

The combined vote for Fine Gael and Fianna Fáil dropped below 50 per cent for the first time: with less than 25,000 votes separating the parties, there could be no stable government that excluded Sinn Féin unless there was a deal between the traditional rivals. The Fianna Fáil leader Micheál Martin chose not to enter a formal 'grand coalition'. Instead, his party supported a government composed of Fine Gael and non-party ministers from outside the cabinet. In the *Irish Times*, Stephen Collins described this arrangement as 'a mechanism for the centre ground of Irish politics to hold on to power without putting Sinn Féin and the hard left in the position of being the only alternative government'.[52]

Breaking the Mould

The combination of a disappointing election result with Syriza's defeat at the hands of the Troika prompted Sinn Féin to modify its rhetoric and positioning as it sought a new way to make progress towards the goal of entering government in Dublin. By January 2017, Gerry Adams was signalling the prospect of a shift in the party's line on coalition: 'I have to say, I never really subscribed to that notion of a left-wing government, certainly not in the short term. I mean, who are the left?'[53] The Sinn Féin Ard Fheis later that year voted to change the policy, opening the door once again to a junior partnership with the centre-right parties. Meanwhile, Adams announced that he would be stepping down as Sinn Féin leader, and Mary Lou McDonald took the reins without a formal leadership contest.

Declan Kearney referred to the new line in oblique terms as he reflected on the conference in *An Phoblacht*:

> We intend to be in government both North and South, to secure and win a unity referendum, and to move towards Irish unity ... Our entry into government in the South will not be dictated by

either Fianna Fáil or Fine Gael but rather by the number of TDs we elect and our future political strength.[54]

For its part, Fianna Fáil emphatically rejected the idea of a coalition with Sinn Féin at the party's 2017 Ard Fheis.[55] The outcome of the local and European elections in May 2019 suggested that there would be no need for either Fianna Fáil or Fine Gael to revisit that stance. Sinn Féin lost nearly half of its council seats and two of its three MEPs, with a drop of almost 8 per cent on its 2014 vote share in the European side of the poll. The Greens more than doubled their vote and came very close to overtaking Sinn Féin as the third-largest force.

Fiach Kelly of the *Irish Times* reported on the concerns of Sinn Féin's would-be coalition partners in a commentary on McDonald's first year as leader: 'Some Fianna Fáilers wonder if a party whose base is built on such a disenfranchised vote will be able to withstand the pressures and compromises of government.'[56] From this perspective, a deal with the Greens seemed like a much safer option, whether it was Fianna Fáil or Fine Gael that held the position of senior coalition partner. After a decade of unprecedented instability, a return to the old two-and-a-half party system appeared to be on the cards, with Sinn Féin diminished and marginalised.

The outcome of the 2020 general election thus came as a tremendous shock to the centre-right parties, the Dublin media and, indeed, Sinn Féin itself. In contrast with the experience of previous elections, support for Sinn Féin rose steadily during the campaign and peaked on election day itself. McDonald's party surged past its rivals and took 24.5 per cent of the vote. Having expected to fight a defensive campaign around the retention of its existing seats, Sinn Féin had not run enough candidates to maximise its representation in the Dáil. Even so, the scale of its achievement was clear. Instead of being able to restore the old political model, with one centre-right party leading the government and another leading the opposition, Fine Gael and Fianna Fáil had to form an outright coalition for the first time in order to exclude Sinn Féin.

The outcome revealed that a large segment of the electorate did not identify with the upbeat narrative of economic recovery that had dominated public discourse in recent years. The gap between that narrative and their own experience was simply too great.[57] Sinn Féin's breakthrough transformed the dynamic of southern politics just as the state was about to enter another profound crisis: the COVID-19 pandemic. The post-crash decade turned Irish politics upside down, placing Sinn Féin at the top of the electoral pecking order. The post-pandemic decade will determine whether the party is able to capitalise on this opportunity by entering government from a position of strength and delivering some of the reforms it has been promising.

NOTES

1. *An Phoblacht* [hereafter *AP*], 16 February 2006.
2. Éirígí, 'Éirígí Becomes a Political Party', 12 May 2007, https://eirigi.org/latestnews/2020/9/29/irg-becomes-a-political-party (all URLs last accessed 3 May 2023).
3. *Ibid.*
4. 'Radical Group Seeks Republican Ground Lost by Sinn Féin', *Irish Times*, 27 July 2009.
5. '€5.3 Billion in Savings and 17,000 Job Cuts Proposed by Review Group', *Irish Times*, 17 July 2009.
6. The National Assets Management Agency (NAMA) was established by the Irish government to operate as a 'bad bank', taking up to €90 billion of land and property development loans off the books of Irish banks.
7. 'For What Died the Sons of Róisín? Smash the NAMA Republic', 12 April 2010, www.indymedia.ie/article/96337.
8. 'Greek Protestors Storm the Acropolis', *The Guardian*, 4 May 2010.
9. 'Protestors Hit at Banks with Rooftop Demo', *Evening Herald*, 15 May 2010.
10. 'Gardai Train in Secret for Riots', *Sunday Independent*, 16 May 2010.
11. 'Republican Mavericks behind City Protest', *Evening Herald*, 19 May 2010.
12. 'Real IRA Says It Will Target UK Bankers', *The Guardian*, 14 September 2010.
13. 'Police Believe Bomb Abandoned by Real IRA Thugs', *Irish Independent*, 6 October 2010.
14. 'Real IRA Admits Bomb Attacks on Northern Ireland Banks', *The Guardian*, 25 October 2011.
15. 'From Socialism Alone Will the Salvation of Ireland Come', Éirígí policy paper, December 2010.
16. 'Workers Pay €50 billion for Bankers' Gambling Debts', 2 October 2010, www.eirigi.org/latest/latest021010.html [Wayback Machine].

17. 'Mary Harney "Blood on Your Hands" Direct Action', 2 November 2010, https://eirigi.org/latestnews/2022/11/2/mary-harney-blood-on-your-hands-direct-action.
18. 'Hijacked: Republican Militants Are Blamed as Students' Peaceful Protest Turns Bloody', *Evening Herald*, 4 November 2011.
19. 'Arrests Due after Protests at Labour's Conference', *Connacht Tribune*, 20 April 2012.
20. 'Dwyer Commits Loyalty to Republican Socialist Group', *New Ross Standard*, 11 September 2012.
21. *AP*, 19 April 2007.
22. *AP*, 10 May 2007.
23. *AP*, 24 May 2007.
24. *AP*, 31 May 2007.
25. *AP*, 14 June 2007.
26. *AP*, 28 June 2007.
27. *AP*, 13 December 2007.
28. *AP*, 6 March 2008.
29. *AP*, 10 January 2008.
30. *AP*, 9 October 2008.
31. *AP*, 22 January 2009; *AP*, 16 April 2009.
32. *AP*, 24 September 2009.
33. *AP*, 26 February 2009.
34. *AP*, 19 March 2009.
35. Stephen Collins, 'Seismic Shift Sends Irish Politics into a New Phase', *Irish Times*, 28 February 2016.
36. Gerry Adams, 'A Bus Ride to Independence and Socialism' (1986), in Gerry Adams, *Signposts to Independence and Socialism* (Dublin: Sinn Féin Publicity Department, 1988), p. 17.
37. *AP*, 2 December 2012.
38. *AP*, 1 April 2015.
39. *AP*, 30 April 2018.
40. *AP*, 1 April 2015. Ó Broin's criticisms of his party's approach were articulated most notably in his book *Sinn Féin and the Politics of Left Republicanism* (London: Pluto Press, 2009), pp. 292–5.
41. *AP*, 1 April 2015.
42. Daniel Finn, 'Ireland's Water Wars', *New Left Review*, September–October 2015, https://newleftreview.org/issues/ii95/articles/daniel-finn-ireland-s-water-wars.
43. Right2Change, 'Policy Principles for a Progressive Irish Government', 2016, www.right2water.ie/sites/default/files/media/Right2Change%20Policies.pdf.
44. Paul Hosford, 'Sinn Féin Accused of "Power Grab" over the Right2Change Pact', *The Journal*, 31 October 2015.

45. Agnes Maillot, 'Sinn Féin's Approach to the EU: Still More "Critical" than "Engaged"?', *Irish Political Studies* 24, no. 4 (2009): 559–74, https://doi.org/10.1080/07907180903274834.
46. *AP*, 30 April 2012.
47. *AP*, 2 February 2015.
48. *AP*, 3 August 2015.
49. *AP*, 3 August 2015.
50. Fiach Kelly, 'Irish Policy on Troika Paid Off, Says Brendan Howlin', *Irish Times*, 27 February 2015.
51. Shaun Connolly, 'A Spoonful of Sugar Helps Medicine Go Down', *Irish Examiner*, 14 October 2015.
52. Stephen Collins, 'Fine Gael and Fianna Fáil Have an Incentive to Deliver Political Stability', *Irish Times*, 7 May 2016.
53. Pat Leahy, 'Gerry Adams Casts Doubt on Future of NI Executive', *Irish Times*, 27 January 2017.
54. *AP*, 27 November 2017.
55. Sarah Bardon, 'Fianna Fáil Members Vote to Block Sinn Féin Coalition', *Irish Times*, 13 October 2017.
56. Fiach Kelly, 'McDonald's Tricky First Year Underlines Sinn Féin's Central Problem', *Irish Times*, 9 February 2019.
57. Terrence McDonough, 'The Irish Economic Model Is Built on Rotten Foundations – Now Its People Want an Alternative', *Jacobin*, 25 October 2020.

11

Conclusion

Oisín Gilmore

Ireland's revolutionary history has inspired radicals all across the world. But, by the start of the twenty-first century, as new head-quarters for Google, Twitter and Facebook were being built on Dublin's derelict docklands, this revolutionary tradition – with its rich tapestry of republican martyrs, militant trade unions, armed struggle and mass civil disobedience – already felt anachronistic. In the place of anti-imperialist guerillas were neoliberal centrists, and in the place of traditional peasantry were urban tech workers.

The economic boom of the Celtic Tiger years saw a sharp rise in household income, and a cultural and political consensus that history had ended and weren't we lucky. No more struggle or conflict, just a peaceful road to economic prosperity and sleepy democracy. No radical change is required when anyone can work hard and get rich.

Opposition to the power of the ruling class had all but disap-peared. The possibility of an alternative to capitalism seemed to have vanished.

Consider the two main historical forces of the left in Ireland: the Labour Party and republicanism. Before the crisis, Labour presented neither a critique of contemporary society nor any alter-native vision of society. Rather, they argued Labour was more aligned with contemporary values than the government; Pat Rabbitte, Labour leader from 2002 to 2007, campaigned on the idea that most people already 'think' Labour but don't vote Labour.[1] What a sharp contrast with Rabbitte's politics from 1986 when, as a Workers' Party politician, he posed a socialist alternative to the Irish people in such militant rhetoric as the following: 'There is no secret about our purpose. It is to win state power for the Irish working class.'² Irish republicans took an equally remarkable path of political moderation. From engaging in an armed revolutionary war with the declared aim of establishing a socialist republic, their ambitions were much reduced in a few short years. By 2005, Sinn Féin president Gerry Adams argued: 'Another world is possible. How is this to be done? Bono and Bob Geldof and other activists have pointed to a different way'.³

In the shadows of this neoliberal consensus, there existed, of course, subterranean strands of radical activism in the campaigns against the water tax and the bin tax, Shell to Sea, the justice for Terence Wheelock campaign, and the anti-globalisation and anti-war movements. However, these were generally fragmentary, ephemeral and marginal.

But when the economic crisis of 2008–10 hit, this cosy consensus broke down. Ireland was rocked both by economic catastrophe and massive political turmoil. Over time, the Irish left moved from a position of irrelevance to a powerful force in Irish politics. This change was not instantaneous or spontaneous. As this book has shown, it developed out of 15 years of social conflict and social movements.

The anti-water charges movement in Ireland was one of the largest social movements of the last 30 years in Britain or Ireland. The movement for abortion rights in Ireland was surely one of the largest feminist movements in a developed country in the last 40 or so years.

In 2016, Trotskyists won nine out of 157 contested parliamentary seats, perhaps the greatest electoral success of Trotskyism in any western country ever. Sinn Féin has gone from winning four seats in the pre-crisis 2007 election, to becoming the most popular party in the country. These are significant movements and significant political developments.

If we were to take any initial lesson from all of this, it is that nothing is predetermined. Nobody in Ireland in 2007 would have imagined that Ireland was going to see these movements or see the development of one of the strongest electoral lefts in western Europe.

However, despite these successes, the left is in many ways as weak as it was pre-2008. No lasting form of working-class self-organisation has emerged. Union density is lower now than it was in 2007. No mass parties have emerged. There are no significant online or offline left publications. Social centres such as Seomra Spraoi have closed down. Though a small number of left bookshops remain, radical spaces still struggle to survive. And while the left has demonstrated a continued ability to mobilise, especially around the Palestine solidarity movement, the mass political engagement of the anti-water tax and repeal movements has dissipated.

Instead, faith is again put in electoral politics. On the margins, People Before Profit continues as a significant organisation, although very dependent on both the income and profile generated from their few Dáil seats. In the main, people are putting most of their faith in the belief that change will be delivered by a Sinn Féin-led government.

Given the electoral success of rightwing populism across Europe, Sinn Féin is unusual. In Ireland its growth is the main electoral story of the last five to ten years. The party campaigns on old-school democratic socialist politics that have become unfashionable for the left in Europe. They promise to engage in a large housebuilding programme, nationalise the healthcare system, significantly cut the costs of childcare and reunite the country – a non-trivial agenda. There is a strong possibility that after the next Dáil election, they will both be the biggest party in the country and lead the next government.

These apparent advances by the left in Ireland contrast sharply with the decline of its counterparts in most of the West. Although the decade after 2008 saw a huge explosion of popular movements, the left today in many countries is in a worse position than it was before the crisis. The movements of the squares have dissipated and is largely only remembered in its various postmortems. The electoral experiments of Syriza, Corbynism and Bernie Sanders all ended in failure. Despite years of struggle involving hundreds of thousands, there are hardly even any reforms or victories to which people can point to show that activism can yield results.

Of course, the problems faced by the left over the last 15 years reflect a longer problem. The crisis of the left in western Europe is nothing new. It has never recovered from the defeats of the 1980s and 1990s. Since then, in almost every country, there has been a decline in the membership of trade unions and parties, the two main institutions of the twentieth-century left. The communist parties of France, Italy and Spain have faded into a shadow of their former strength. Social democratic and democratic socialist parties have almost all shifted sharply to the right and seen a dramatic fall in their memberships and vote shares. Beyond electoral politics, in many countries the trade union movement is weaker than at any point in the last 100 years, while, as a counter-hegemonic cultural project, the left has almost disappeared.

The advance of the left in Ireland is even more striking when the political situation in pre-crisis Ireland is compared with that of other western European states. As described in the introduction to this volume, Ireland has long more resembled other post-colonial states than western European ones, with left politics being pursued through the anti-imperialist republican movement. Unlike in most European states, the socialist movement has never taken state power.

This conclusion aims to examine the Irish left in comparison with the western European left, looking at their similarities and differences. Given the apparent success of the Irish left and the apparent failure of the western European left in recent years, it asks if this example of success shows a route out of the long-standing crisis of the western European left. To begin addressing this, it is worth examining how the western European left got into the state it is currently in.

THE WESTERN LEFT TODAY

After the Second World War, governments across western Europe were elected through recently established universal suffrage, and the organs of the left – its parties and unions – gave their members real power and an ability to directly affect the future development of society. Through the incorporation of once marginal workers organisations into the administration of capitalism, they grew into truly mass organisations as more and more workers joined. But over time, as they took on the role of improving the governance and administration of capitalism, the question of socialist trans-formation became less important for these socialist organisations.

And, with its increased administrative focus, the organisational base of the left eroded.

As left organisations became increasingly dependent on university-educated experts, access to power became increasingly professionalised.[4] The space for worthwhile grassroots activism in unions and socialist parties shrank and with that membership fell. In a process that the political scientist Peter Mair called cartelisation, parties became increasingly integrated into the state and the self-reproduction of a technocratic social elite, with less and less need for a membership base or even a support base outside of the occasional election.[5]

Between the late 1970s and early 1990s, the 'forward march' of the twentieth-century left ground to a halt.[6] And, arising from the political defeats and economic restructuring that took place between the 1970s and 1990s, the twentieth-century left entered a period of crisis, from which it never recovered. Over the last 50 years, both western capitalism and the left have been transformed through the combined effect of: the fall of the apparent alternative economic arrangement in the Soviet Union; several major defeats in industrial disputes; financialisaton and the globalisation of finance; de-industrialisation; and the increased casualisation of work. Gone are both the democratic mass organisations and the participative, democratic culture that defined the left for much of the twentieth century.

Increasingly, power and responsibility were shifted away from democratic institutions – parties, unions and even parliaments and councils – and transferred to professionals, experts, technocrats, NGOs and transnational institutions. For many years the left fought for people to be able to control their own lives, first by struggling for legal equality and elected government, then for democratic social control over the means of production. But as these collective goals became increasingly unattainable, the consolation prize was individual rights.

A new politics developed where the virtue of western democracies was no longer the system of personal freedom and self-government but, rather, 'free markets' combined with technocratic government that ensured good living conditions for all. This era of post-political liberalism lasted for close to 20 years.

While the professionalised centre-left of the 1990s did oversee two decades of economic and political stability,[7] its overall project must be seen as a complete failure. It did not lead to prosperity. Rather this period saw ever-increasing wealth and income inequality. As the rich and powerful grew richer and more powerful, ordinary people were increasingly politically disenfranchised and disengaged while experiencing stagnant or even falling living standards. And on an international stage, it did not lead to a world order based on peace and respect for international human rights. Rather, these very centrists launched a war of conquest killing hundreds of thousands in Iraq and today they wave on a genocide in Gaza.

All the while, at the margins of society, the socialist left persisted. With the decline of the twentieth-century left, it faced a dilemma over what to do. Some tried to rebuild the left of the late twentieth-century, with its socialist or communist parties and trade unions.[8] Some instead argued that the left needed to return to its roots and tried to rebuild an autonomous workers' movement like the revolutionary syndicalists of the early twentieth century.[9] Others simply continued as though nothing had changed. Many Trotskyists continued to criticise the leadership of the centre-left for being bad socialists even when the centre-left no longer claimed to be socialist at all. Others continued as lone voices in increasingly closed centre-left political spaces. Unexpectedly, it was often these remnants of the left of the 1970s – Jeremy Corbyn, Bernie Sanders and Jean-Luc Mélenchon – that provided the strongest party-political base for the left in the years after the crisis.

For the tiny number that were involved in radical left politics before the great financial crisis, it was clear they were engaged in a form of politics incapable of realising its own aims. They accepted that class struggle had entered a downturn and that they were in a period of political moderation. But they held out in the belief that, because of the class nature of capitalist society, at some stage class struggle would re-emerge. And this would see the re-emergence of working-class self-organisation and provide a space for the activity of the radical left.

However, while, in response to the great financial crisis, class struggle did re-emerge, the type of self-organisation and tactics that the radical left was expecting did not. Changing forms of social and political organisation, and the new power of the internet, led to massive explosions of protestors with loose organisation and connections, and vague demands that were not directed towards any institution that might be able or willing to implement them.

In the years following the 2008 crisis, mass social movements emerged all across the world, reaching an apogee in the 2010–2012 period. Among these were the Tahrir Square protests, the 2010 student protests and 2011 riots in Britain, Gezi Park in Turkey, the 15-M/Indignados movement in Spain, the anti-austerity movement in Greece, Movimento Passe Livre in Brazil and Occupy in America spreading throughout the world. In retrospect, these movements look like a series of failures. While some had clear demands,[10] many movements in this period, in particular in Europe, did not go beyond the rejection of the technocratic elite and vague calls for things like 'real democracy', which could act as a stand in for anything from anarchist communism to far-right ethno-nationalism. Even worse, at times these movements released counter-revolutionary forces – such as in Brazil and Egypt – which they had no ability to control.[11]

A striking aspect of these movements was the focus on 'occupying' what was already public space, most obviously in the Occupy movement, but also seen in the wider 'movement of the squares' that involved the occupation of Puerta del Sol in Madrid, Plaça Catalunya in Barcelona and Syntagma Square in Athens. All these presented a novel form of political activity based around a long-running occupation of a major town square.

Perhaps, the most noticeable feature of the 2010 movements was how these mobilisations were organised. Nearly always they involved a very light form of organisation where a few committed activists used social media to mobilise large numbers. They were less a story of mass organisation than mass mobilisation. Where organisation existed, it was light and frequently ephemeral. On almost no occasion did these movements penetrate from public spaces into the private spaces of capitalist production through any form of worker mobilisation, never mind workplace organisation. This was partly due to the changing nature of work. It makes sense that workers in dispersed, casualised service sector work would not organise through workplace assemblies, like those seen in the late 1960s and 1970s. What would a workplace assembly look like in a Starbucks or a call centre? Rather, we might imagine that for these workers, gathering together to collectively discuss their common problems might take the form of a public assembly – like the kind seen during the aforementioned movements of the squares.

This organisational pattern was fuelled by the mobilising ability of the internet. Social media made it easier to mobilise large numbers, but it was far more difficult to integrate them into any long-lasting organisation. While these movements often voiced clear politics of opposition and often succeeded in creating an experience of communal resistance, they rarely succeeded in winning reforms or even in articulating clear achievable demands.

The movements that flourished in the years since 2008 have been large but ephemeral. They have failed to lay deep social roots. They have failed to build sustainable organisations. They have failed to identify an avenue through which society might be changed, and given this, they have failed to develop a mass political conscious-ness around the capitalist nature of our society or around what needs to be done to change it. As such, while they have frequently terrified the ruling elite, they have never presented a serious chal-lenge to the existing order.

Ireland

In some ways, a similar process played out in Ireland; previous protest repertoires such as strikes and boycotts were largely aban-doned. There were occasional workplace occupations, but these were few and occurred mainly in the early years of the crisis. While the traditional repertoire of marching to the Dáil continued, the small numbers at these demonstrations, once austerity was being overseen by the ECB, IMF and European Commission, spoke of the futility of marching to an institution that was taking its own marching orders from elsewhere. Irish people showed an instinc-tive understanding of the hollowing out of institutions which Peter Mair had spoken of. Nevertheless, the small marches continued to the Dáil. However futile they were, it would have been even more futile to protest the unresponsive, unrepresentative foreign institutions that were driving austerity in Ireland.

Missing in Ireland, especially in the early years, were the massive explosions of protest seen in other countries during 2009–13. There were pale attempts to replicate movements seen from afar by the far-left parties and by those in Occupy, but they failed to capture imaginations or spread. Considering the outcome of such unfocused disorganised anger, and how these movements were sidelined or occasionally taken over by rightwing anti-democratic forces, this was maybe no bad thing.[12]

One event in Ireland that appeared to resemble these spontaneous explosions – the first water charges protest in October 2014 – actually speaks of the differences. This protest had been built up for many months and was jealously curated by institutional actors – left parties and unions – who therefore managed to maintain focus on their central demand and not have the protests spin out of control. This type of difference may be one reason why, unlike other countries, there are at least three identifiable victories by the left in Ireland over the last 15 years.

The first two are the easiest to identify. Firstly, through a massive and militant struggle involving huge levels of grassroots engagement and struggle, the attempted imposition of water charges was defeated. Secondly, through a long struggle over years, the right to abortion was won.

Trickier to identify, but unquestionably real, is the fact that Ireland is a more leftwing country than it was in 2007. For instance, between the summer of 2021 and the summer of 2024, the left consistently outpolled the right, whereas before 2008, the left only had a third of the support for rightwing parties.[13]

If we take housing as an example, we can see how attitudes have changed. Pre-crisis, the consensus was that the state has only a minor ameliorative role in the housing market, and instead should focus on creating the correct incentives for private developers to 'solve' the housing crisis through the market. In contrast, today the consensus is that there is a need for far greater state involvement in the housing market, and for large-scale state-led housebuilding projects, and this is currently being advanced by even the right-coalition of Fine Gael, Fianna Fáil and the Greens.

Or, if we consider the arena of international politics, it is largely because of the strength of the left that, after the start of Israel's assault on Gaza in 2023, the current centre-right government in Dublin quickly called for Israel to declare a ceasefire and began to explore its trade links with Israel. Some explain Ireland being an outlier on this question with reference to its anti-imperialist history, which contrasts starkly with the imperialist history of many of Israel's cheerleaders. There is some truth to that, but the Republic of Ireland had previously been happy to stay within the pro-Israel EU consensus. A lot has changed.

While, the material successes of the Irish left and its social movements have been unique, there have been, of course, many ways in which the experience in Ireland has mirrored those of western Europe. The same structural changes that are happening across western Europe with regards to the media landscape, the nature of work, and the rise of technocratic government are happening in Ireland as well.

But there are also significant differences, in particular, there were significant differences between the left in Ireland and internationally. In advance of the crisis, the left in Ireland was in a rather different position to the left in many other countries. In many western countries, the socialist and social democratic left, after dominating the politics of the twentieth century, was directionless and dying, as its social base in a large manufacturing workforce seemed to be in terminal decline. In Ireland, as discussed in the introduction, the socialist left was never dominant. Ireland had never had the large industrial workforce seen in other western European countries. The result of this was that there was significantly less nostalgia or disorientation on the Irish left in the early 2000s than there might have been in other countries.

In fact, in some ways, the left in Ireland was well prepared for the crisis. The kind of identity-centred politics that pointed away from economic issues and towards cultural questions had not become dominant on the radical left in Ireland in the way it had in many other countries. And the left approached the crisis with certain organisational repertoires that proved useful in the 2000s. The organisational practices around the Shell to Sea campaign and in the libertarian end of the left provided an activist expertise that enabled the organisation of the Abortion Right Campaign between 2012 and 2018, and of the housing movement. And the successful struggle against the water tax in the 1990s provided a blueprint for how it could be done again in the 2013–16 movement.

While Ireland did see some 'Occupy' camps in 2011, square occupations did not play the role they did in many other countries. This is likely largely down to the weather, and also the perceived futility of such camps in a peripheral country. But other features of the post-2008 period did emerge, if only fleetingly so.

Like those in New York, Madrid and Athens, many expressed their politics in terms of a rejection of a technocratic elite, while very few beyond the core, committed activists presented a critique of capitalism. There was a widespread sense of betrayal and indignation. And there was a desperate grasping for claims to rights and democracy that seemed oddly devoid of content.

But, of the many movements in Ireland during the 15 years since 2008, the most important two were organised around clear achievable demands. This contrasts with recent movements in other countries, which often failed to articulate such well-defined short-term goals. The movement for abortion rights campaigned explicitly and unambiguously for the repeal of the Eighth Amendment to the constitution and legislation for 'free, safe and legal' abortion. The movement against the water tax wanted water domestic water supply to be publicly owned and financed through general taxation. It was evident to all what the movements wanted and how they could be achieved. And in both cases the movements definitively won the core issues of the campaigns.

These social movements had strong roots in Ireland. The movement against the water tax organised on a grassroots community basis. The abortion right movement had a very large and vocal support base, in particular among young women.

However, while these movements were deeply rooted, like those in other countries they were fleeting. A simple overwhelming fact is no durable mass organisations emerged out of the struggles of the last 15 years.

The Abortion Rights Campaign was a well organised democratic membership-based organisation. But, after winning its core demands it has developed from a large activist organisation into a small campaign group, which lobbies for better abortion services. The aspirations of many members of the time, that the energies and organisation of the movement be channelled into a more general feminist movement, have simply not come to pass.

The anti-water charges movement, while supported by unions and left parties, was based largely on locally organised groups that had a loose connection with the national Right2Water campaign. While both the national campaign and the local groups were well organised, they did not form a unified democratic organisation in the style of the Abortion Right Campaign. With the victory of the campaigns, the movement did not develop into anything lasting. The attempt to turn the Right2Water campaign into an electoral coalition or into a new party was met with indifference by the political groupings involved and the wider public. And the local campaign groups largely disappeared.

Over this period, the trade union movement continued in its decline. No mass parties have emerged. Though People Before Profit has emerged as a significant party on the left, it remains very small and very dependent on its elected members, with weak local organisation outside of areas with locally respected elected representatives.

A striking feature of the rise of Sinn Féin is how their rise has not involved the kind of membership growth seen by other left electoral initiatives, such as the explosion in membership of the UK Labour Party under Corbyn. Although their membership has grown in recent years, the party remains relatively small. In 2020, their stated membership was 15,000, when Fianna Fáil and Fine Gael had 20,000 and 25,000 members respectively.[14] Since then, it would appear that their membership in the south has declined.[15]

Like other countries, with the decline of parties, trade unions and left media outlets, political education within social movements has often been quite poor. Many do not develop any analysis of the nature of social problems or what their solutions might be. Instead, as in other countries, analysis often remains at the level of observing that we are increasingly governed by an unaccountable technocratic elite and proposing unclear ideas like 'real democracy'.

AFTER THE MOVEMENTS

There are perhaps two key findings from this book about the left in Ireland since 2008. Firstly, that the 2008–18 period saw the emergence of major mass movements that have both fundamentally changed Ireland's political life and can provide lessons for the left internationally. Secondly, that the electoral rise of Sinn Féin and the left more broadly is almost entirely a reflection of the change brought about by the movements of the 2008–18 period. These are positive lessons, but the obvious question remains: what has happened to social movements since 2018?

From the left, there has been the steady development of a housing movement, most impressively in the development of the Community Action Tenants Union (CATU), as described in Chapter 5. In more recent months there has been a very large and impressive movement in solidarity with Palestine. This movement has organised multiple demonstrations with tens of thousands in attendance. It is estimated up to 80,000 people attended a demonstration in Dublin on 19 February 2024, making it the largest demonstration in Dublin since the water tax demonstrations in 2014–16.[16]

As has been stated, the left is in a strong position. And it is possible that for the first time since the civil war, there will be a left-led government in Ireland. But unfortunately, there are many reasons to temper any optimism.

For the first time since the mid-twentieth century, a significant far-right movement has developed in the southern 26 counties. This movement emerged from the coalescing of a number of political tendencies around opposition to the COVID-19 lockdowns. Central to this were radicalised far-right 'Christians' who had campaigned against the repeal of the Eighth Amendment. They were joined by conspiracy-theory elements that had been on the fringes of anti-austerity movements since the beginning of the recession, whether in Occupy, the anti-water tax movement, in more explicitly rightwing groups such as freemen-on-the-land or Direct Democracy Ireland or simply as a growing cohort of isolated young men who took their Americanised understanding of shadowy forces controlling the world from a radicalising internet manosphere.

After the decade of mass movement, many of these had some experience in organising street movements and using social media to mobilise people. The COVID-19 lockdowns in Ireland were largely based on popular consent, and thus the small anti-lockdown protests, despite clearly being in breach of the law, were largely tolerated. Because most on the left were in support of the COVID-19 lockdowns, believing they were a necessary health measure, almost no leftwing meetings or demonstrations and very little organisation took place from March 2020 until the second half of 2021, when the initial vaccination programme was finally complete. The tiny far right in Ireland enjoyed more or less free rein to organise and build a base through the anti-lockdown movement, providing the only voice of real opposition to lockdowns in this period.

By 2022, there was a growing number of far-right activists in Ireland, with a small core effectively acting as full-time activists. They mobilised against the LGBT+ community, attacking libraries that stocked sexual health books aimed at LGBT+ teenagers. And they attacked and even burned down buildings being used to house asylum seekers. While initially this was a small movement, in November 2022 there was an unexpectedly large demonstration in the community of East Wall in Dublin against the use of a vacant office block to house asylum seekers. Since then, there have been over 100 local protests against the use of local buildings to house asylum seekers, with over 20 arson attacks on these buildings. While these demonstrations have generally been very small, rarely with more than 100, they have been widespread across many towns and villages. In November 2023, a mentally ill homeless Algerian man, who had lived in Ireland for 20 years, attacked a group of children outside a city centre school with a knife, critically injuring a five-year-old girl. The far right used this horrific attack as an opportunity to mobilise an anti-immigrant riot, which caused widespread destruction in Dublin city centre. The far right has also harassed, issued death threats to, and even assaulted a number of left politicians. And, in March 2024, a Croatian carpenter, Josip Štrok, was beaten to death in Clondalkin, Dublin, apparently simply because he was not speaking English. Then, in the June 2024 local elections, five far-right candidates were elected, including one candidate from the neo-Nazi 'National Party'.

The rise of the far right since 2018 has been a shock. Previous attempts at far-right organising in Ireland have for decades been forcefully opposed by the left. For example, in 2016, an attempt to organise an Irish version of the German Islamophobic PEGIDA[17] group was defeated when, in February of that year, thousands of anti-racist demonstrators filled the centre of town, preventing PEGIDA from assembling there, while outside this central area, militant anti-fascists from anarchist, socialist and republican backgrounds physically attacked PEGIDA supporters spotted around town. That was the end of PEGIDA in Ireland.

Historically, anti-fascism in Ireland has a long and impressive history of nipping in the bud any attempt to organise by Ireland's tiny far right. However, COVID-19 gave the far right something of an incubation period, and since then they have proven far harder to address. While these developments are daunting and terrifying, the fascist core of this movement remains very small and socially marginal. While there remains little support for these far-right groups, their success lies firstly in getting more mainstream parties to repeat key parts of their rhetoric about restricting immigration and fighting cultural wars. Secondly it lies in diverting anger away from government authorities and businesses towards the vulnerable – housing shortages are seen less and less as a result of government failure or predatory vulture funds, and more as an effect of immigration. Although there is time to reverse the rise of the far right, it is already creating problems for the left. This can be seen in the 2024 European elections, where the far right gained a few seats, while Sinn Féin and the rest of the left performed worse than expected.

Looking Forward

In many ways, despite the victories of the left since 2008, the future looks bleak. While a Sinn Féin-led government offers the prospect of real change with a major housebuilding programme, an Irish NHS, reunification and significant investment in public services, a question remains: can it deliver? While it has clear policies for radical change in a number of areas, most strikingly housing and reunification, in many other areas its plans are much less developed – including on central issues for the left such as climate change, workers' rights and the European Union. Perhaps more concerningly, it is increasingly not campaigning on concrete plans for change – but instead on vaguer commitments for 'change' and promising to 'fix the housing crisis'. It is hard to believe Sinn Féin will deliver the change that many desire or fix the housing crisis within a single government term. If it fails to deliver and fails to significantly improve the lives of its voters, where does its support go? It is unlikely the Trotskyist People Before Profit will manage to articulate a viable alternative. And it is hard to see a surge in support for the two centre-left parties, Labour and the Social Democrats, who currently appeal mainly to middle-class professionals. Worryingly, the far right could easily make inroads.

Looking back, the achievements of the social movements since 2008 are striking. There are some real, substantial victories. Hundreds of thousands were mobilised. And the political culture of Ireland was definitely changed. The neoliberal consensus of the 1990s and 2000s is over. While the left has always played a central role in Ireland's struggle against British imperialism, it was always marginal in the politics of the southern post-colonial state. Today, the left in Ireland is no longer marginal. While in almost all of Europe the last few decades have witnessed the decline of the left, in Ireland it has grown in strength.

These movements have demonstrated what can be achieved. They have shown how when movements identify what they want to win and how they can win it, they can be victorious. They have shown how, despite the decline of the left all across the west, successful social struggles that win can build support for the left and for a project of social change.

But looking forward, the achievements of the last 15 years seem rather more fragmented: the defeat of a relatively small water tax; the achievement of abortion rights decades after the rest of western Europe; mobilisations that failed to result in lasting organisation; and electoral gains arising from a period of struggle that is now very much in the rear-view mirror.

There is today in Ireland significant support for the left and a progressive project of social change, but what that means is unclear not only to wider society but for the left itself. There have been fragments of victories, and, with the possibility of a major project of building public housing, there is the prospect of another major victory. But how does it fit together? How do these separate parts fit together into a wider project of social change? The left is unable to answer.

For the far right, the answer is easier. They say we need to expunge those who are corrupting the nation, whether it be politicians, immigrants, LGBT+ people or the left. They say once these cancers have been excised, social problems will fade away. To state the obvious, such a project is doomed to fail. Problems in society do not arise from contamination and will not be resolved through expunging. All the far right will deliver is increased misery. But they provide easy answers – the problem is casually identified as a group in society, and getting rid of that group or putting it under foot is not only an easily understood solution but one that can easily be imagined being implemented.

For the left, the problem is harder. We may be able to identify the problem – that we live in a society organised to ensure investors earn healthy profits rather than to satisfy human needs. The solution might be equally clear, that production needs to be put under democratic social control. But the steps between the current situation and the long-term goal of socialism are less clear than ever before. Ireland has demonstrated that short-term victories can be won and what that can do for the left. But the medium term is missing.

Ireland's experience provides a lesson to the wider European left that any victories, however fragmented, are worth fighting for. It is possible to win, and winning is what matters. But, as the last 15 years are looked at in the rear-view mirror, and we try to look ahead, it is clear that fragments of victory are not enough.

NOTES

1. Alison O'Connor, 'We Were Right Not to Go into Government, says Rabbitte', *Irish Independent*, 23 December 2002, www.independent. ie/irish-news/we-were-right-not-to-go-into-government-says-rabbitte/26025116.html (last accessed 28 June 2024) and Gene McKenna, 'Rabbitte Rounds Up Young Guns to Take on "Arrogant" Coalition', *Irish Independent*, 12 May 2003, www.independent.ie/irish-news/rabbitte-

rounds-up-young-guns-to-take-on-arrogant-coalition/25946687.html (last accessed 28 June 2024).

2. Brian Hanley and Scott Millar, *The Lost Revolution: The Story of the Official IRA and the Workers' Party* (London: Penguin, 2009), p. 450.

3. Gerry Adams, *The New Ireland: A Vision for the Future* (Kerry: Brandon Books, 2005), p. 21.

4. Stephanie L. Mudge, *Leftism Reinvented: Western Parties from Socialism to Neoliberalism* (Cambridge, MA: Harvard University Press, 2018).

5. Peter Mair, *Ruling the Void: The Hollowing of Western Democracy* (London: Verso, 2023).

6. Eric Hobsbawm, 'The Forward March of Labour Halted?', *Marxism Today*, September 1978.

7. Ben S. Bernanke, 'The Great Moderation', remarks at the meetings of the Eastern Economic Association, Washington DC, 20 February 2004, www.federalreserve.gov/boarddocs/speeches/2004/20040220/ (last accessed 28 June 2024).

8. Here we can think of party initiatives such as Rifondazione Comunista or the Scottish Socialist Party, and union initiatives such as the RMT under Bob Crow or the various iteration of the 'organising model' that have been promoted over the last 30 years.

9. Here we can point to the revival of anarchism and anarcho-syndicalism in the late 1990s and early 2000s. See: Immanuel Ness (ed.), *New Forms of Worker Organization: The Syndicalist and Autonomist Restoration of Class-Struggle Unionism* (Oakland, CA: PM Press, 2014).

10. See, for example, the call for the resignation of Mubarak in Egypt, the opposition to the increases in student fees and the abolition of the Education Maintenance Allowance in the UK, or the call for free public transport in Brazil.

11. Vincent Bevins, *If We Burn: The Mass Protest Decade and the Missing Revolution* (London: Hachette UK, 2023).

12. *Ibid.*

13. Despite the left consistently outpolling the right for four years, in the June 2024 local elections, the combined vote for rightwing parties was 53 per cent against a combined vote for leftwing parties of 25 per cent. A slight decline on the left's performance in the 2019 local elections, when the combined vote for rightwing parties was 54 per cent against a combined vote for leftwing parties of 26 per cent. Whether this will translate into a poor performance for the left in the upcoming general elections remains to be seen. For a list of which parties were counted as right and left see note 12 in Chapter 1.

14. Colm Keena, 'Sinn Féin is the Richest Political Party in Ireland', *Irish Times*, 5 March 2020, www.irishtimes.com/news/politics/sinn-fein-is-the-richest-political-party-in-ireland-1.4193124 (last accessed 28 June 2024).

15. Philip Ryan, 'Sinn Féin's Revenue from Membership Fees Slumps Despite Record Poll Ratings', *Irish Independent*, 13 October 2022, www.independent.ie/irish-news/politics/sinn-feins-revenue-from-membership-fees-slumps-despite-record-poll-ratings/42062953.html (last accessed 28 June 2024).

16. Beatrice Fanucci, '80,000 People Attend Palestine Solidarity March in Dublin Calling for Gaza Ceasefire', *GCN (Gay Community News)*, 19 February 2024, https://gcn.ie/palestine-solidarity-march-dublin-gaza-ceasefire/ (last accessed 28 June 2024).

17. PEGIDA is a German acronym for Patriotische Europäer Gegen die Islamisierung des Abendlandes (Patriotic Europeans Against the Islamisation of the West). The Irish group used the German acronym.

Notes on Contributors

Paul Dillon is a graduate of University College Dublin (UCD) and the Dublin Institute of Technology (DIT). He holds master's degrees in political science and journalism and is currently a PhD candidate at the University of Limerick. He is a former president of the UCD Students Union. He was twice elected as a member of the national executive committee of the Labour Party (2007 to 2010). He is also a former political director of the Social Democrats.

Kevin Doyle was one of the founders of the anarchist Workers Solidarity Movement in 1984. He has been active in countless campaigns in Cork and nationally over the intervening 40 years. He is also a novelist and his professional page can be found at kevindoyle.ie.

Seamus Farrell is a housing activist who has taken part in community organising and major occupations in Dublin since the Bolt Hostel. He is a founding member of Dublin Central Housing Action and the Community Action Tenants Union (CATU), currently organising in Belfast, North Ireland. He has a PhD from Dublin City University (DCU), Ireland, on the topic of 'A Political Economy of Radical Media', and co-edited *Radical Journalism: Resurgence, Reform, Reaction* (2023).

Daniel Finn is Features Editor for *Jacobin* and the author of *One Man's Terrorist: A Political History of the IRA* (2019). He holds a doctorate in Irish history from University College Cork and has written for a number of publications about Irish and British politics, including *New Left Review, Le Monde Diplomatique* and the *London Review of Books*.

Dave Gibney was co-founder and Campaign Coordinator of Right2Water. He also served as the spokesman of Right2Change. He is currently strategic communications and research officer at Mandate Trade Union, where he has worked since 2013.

Oisín Gilmore is Senior Economist at TASC (Thinktank for Action on Social Change) where he has responsibility for research on economic policy and economic inequality. He has participated in various social movements in Ireland, Britain and continental Europe.

Aisling Hedderman is a founding member of North Dublin Bay Housing Crisis Committee and the Community Action Tenants Union (CATU). She was deeply involved in housing actions after the crash in response to rising homelessness and changing policy around homelessness. Since Ireland's austerity years, she has taken actions which includes local anti-evictions campaigns, the Apollo House and Take Back the City occupations and demonstrations. She is currently the Education Coordinator at CATU and holds an honours degree in social policy and sociology with extensive experience and interest in contemporary housing policy at local and national level.

David Landy is Assistant Professor in the Department of Sociology in Trinity College Dublin and director of the MPhil in Race, Ethnicity, Conflict. He is active in Palestine solidarity, a former chair of the Ireland Palestine Solidarity Campaign and has written on water charges, anti-racism movements and solidarity campaigning in Ireland. He is co-editor of *Enforcing Silence: Academic Freedom and Criticism of Israel* (2020).

Damian Lawlor is an activist, writer and athletics coach. He is the author of *Na Fianna Éireann and the Irish Revolution: 1909–1923* (2009).

Rosi Leonard has played a major role in the recent housing rights movement, in particular in Home Sweet Home and the Apollo House occupation and in Community Action Tenants Union (CATU). She has also worked in youth work and youth arts in Dublin, Glasgow and London. She is currently employed as Network Development Coordinator with Friends of the Earth Ireland.

Dr Mary Muldowney is a Dublin City Council historian in residence. She is co-editor of *Saothar,* the journal of the Irish Labour

History Society (ILHS), and is also a member of the ILHS organising committee. Mary was a SIPTU activist in Trinity College Dublin and she also spent some years training shop stewards for a number of trade unions. Among other labour movement activities, she is one of the organisers of the Robert Tressell Festival, which is based on the themes raised by *The Ragged Trousered Philanthropists*. She is the author of monographs, journal articles and book chapters, primarily devoted to labour history.

Máire Ní Chuagáin is a feminist and activist from Dublin. She has worked for over a decade on issues of social and global justice, and was an active member of the Abortion Rights Campaign from 2017 to 2020.

Aileen O'Carroll has been an activist in the Irish abortion rights movement from the Dublin Abortion Rights Group in the early 1990s up to the more recent Abortion Rights Campaign and the Together 4 Yes campaign. She was also a central member of the Workers Solidarity Movement. She is co-author of *What Worked? How Abortions Activists in Ireland Organised for Victory* (2020), author of *Working Time, Knowledge Work and Post-Industrial Society* (2015) and, with Don Bennett, *The Dublin Docker: Working Lives of Dublin's Deep-Sea Port* (2017). She is Policy Manager at the Digital Repository of Ireland (DRI).

Stewart Reddin is a former regional organiser for Sinn Féin in Dublin. He was a member of Éirígí from its founding in 2006 until 2012 and has since been involved in various political campaigns and community history projects.

Juliana Sassi has been involved in migrants, housing and international solidarity movements in Ireland since 2016. She is a former member of Dublin Central Housing Action and a member of Community Action Tenants Union (CATU). She is a PhD candidate in the Geography Department at Maynooth University, where she researches housing financialisation, corporate landlords and tenants relations. She has developed research on tenants' experiences of home during the COVID-19 pandemic and about the housing movement in Ireland.

Index